Serving Purpose

Transforming mediocracy into excellent STEWARDSHIP

How to effectively STEWARD your Time, Talent & Treasure

Alexander O. Emoghene

Copyright © 2023 Alexander O. Emoghene.

All rights reserved. No part of this book may be reproduced, stored, or transmitted by any means—whether auditory, graphic, mechanical, or electronic—without written permission of both publisher and author, except in the case of brief excerpts used in critical articles and reviews. Unauthorized reproduction of any part of this work is illegal and is punishable by law.

CONTENTS

Introduction v
Acknowledgment ix

PART 1

Chapter 1   Stewardship 1
Chapter 2   Stewardship Connection To Time, Talent, And Treasure 4
Chapter 3   Time 7
Chapter 4   The Limited Nature Of Time 16

PART 2

Chapter 5   Talents 27
Chapter 6   Motivation For Deploying Talents 39
Chapter 7   Understanding Grace Gifts 47

PART 3

Chapter 8	Stewardship Of Treasure	71
Chapter 9	What Is Kingdom Treasure?	79
Chapter 10	Nature Of Kingdom Treasures	88
Chapter 11	Stewardship Boosters	103

Conclusion...121

INTRODUCTION

WELCOME TO THE exciting journey of exploring the principles and practices of stewardship: God's call for us to responsibly manage and utilise the resources in which He entrusted us. This book will delve into the resources of Time, Talent, and Treasure, seeking to understand how we can be faithful stewards in every aspect of our lives.

Embedded deeply within the Scriptures, stewardship emerges as a profound concept, reflecting the very essence of God's heart for His creation and His sincere desire to all humanity to flourish. Throughout the Scriptures, the term "steward" is interchangeably used with "minister" or "servant." All these terms find their origins in the Greek word "oikonomia," which encompasses household management, administration, arrangement, and distribution, including the responsible dispensation of wealth and property.

Yet, stewardship goes beyond financial management; it encompasses a wise and purposeful approach to life. It involves the intentional utilization of our Time, the cultivation and deployment of our Talents, and the careful stewardship of both our spiritual and material possessions. At its core, stewardship acknowledges God's sovereign ownership over all aspects of life, compelling us to embrace our role as caretakers and managers of His blessings for the continual prosperity of humanity. It is a holistic perspective that harmonizes with the divine design for creation and our place within it."

In this book, we will embark on a transformative journey of exploration, reflection, and practical application. We will dive into the biblical principles of stewardship, drawing wisdom from the Word of God and discovering how we can align our lives with His divine purposes.

We will start our journey by examining the stewardship of Time. Time is a precious resource, a currency of life that cannot be earned or saved. It is a gift given to each of us in equal measure, and our responsibility is to use it wisely. We will explore the unique nature of Time and its significance in our lives, recognising the limited nature of Time and the importance of making intentional choices that honor God.

Moving forward, we will delve into the stewardship of talent. Each of us is uniquely gifted by God, endowed with specific abilities and strengths. We will explore discovering, developing, and deploying our skills for God's glory. We will examine the biblical teachings on spiritual gifts and the importance of using our talents to serve others and advance His kingdom.

Lastly, we will explore the stewardship of treasure, material possessions, and resources entrusted to us. We will delve into the biblical principles of financial stewardship, recognizing that all we have is ultimately a blessing from God. We will explore the concept of generosity, wise financial management, and the biblical call to use our resources to bless others and further God's work on earth.

Throughout this book, we will encounter relevant Scripture passages, engage in reflective exercises, and engage in discussions to deepen our understanding and application of stewardship principles. Our goal is not merely to gain knowledge but to be transformed by renewing our minds, resulting in practical and meaningful life changes.

As we embark on this stewardship journey, let us open our hearts to the leading of the Holy Spirit, allowing Him to mold and shape us into faithful stewards. May our Time, talents, and treasures be surrendered to God's purposes, bringing glory to His name and impacting the lives of others.

Are you ready to embark on this exciting adventure of stewardship? Let us dive in together and discover the abundant blessings of faithfully managing and utilising the resources entrusted to us by our loving and generous God.

ACKNOWLEDGMENT

WITH BOUNDLESS LOVE and profound gratitude to the Lord for graciously selecting me to wholeheartedly serve in the ministry, and my utmost admiration for my beloved wife Judith, whose patient attentiveness to the time I devote to prayer and writing fills me with awe. My heartfelt thanks to every individual I have been honored to serve in various capacities; this experience has indelibly fueled my fervor to purposefully serve, propelling me forward on this meaningful and honored journey.

PART 1

CHAPTER

STEWARDSHIP

STEWARDSHIP IN THE Kingdom recognises and understands that everything we have, including our Time, Talents, and Treasures, belongs to God. As kingdom citizens, we are called to manage and utilise these resources in a way that aligns with God's purposes and brings Him glory. Stewardship goes beyond mere ownership; it involves a deep sense of responsibility and accountability to God.

As Kingdom stewards of Time, Talent, and Treasures, we are called to recognise the significance of each moment and make intentional choices about how we spend our days, weeks, and years. Just as we are called to be good stewards of our finances, talents, and other resources, we are also called to be good stewards of the time we have been given.

Understanding the brevity and uncertainty of life, as highlighted in verses like **Psalm 90:12**, *"Teach us to number our days, that we may gain a heart of wisdom,"* we are encouraged to make the most of our time. This involves aligning our attitude, actions, and activities with our values, goals, and priorities that reflect our faith and relationship with God.

Stewardship involves several vital principles and practices:

Prioritization: In our journey towards fulfilling God's purpose for our life in the kingdom, prioritization takes center stage. It encompasses the vital task of recognizing what truly matters and warrants our utmost dedication and commitment. By consciously deciding how we invest our Time, Talent, and Treasure, we can strike a harmonious balance that extends to vital aspects such as our relationship with God, family, work, relationships, personal growth, and rest.

Management: Throughout this book, I will frequently discuss management using various terms and examples, yet they all converge on the fundamental concept of stewardship. We can optimize our time, talents, and treasure by implementing practical biblical management principles. This encompasses the creation of schedules, to-do lists, and the establishment of goals. Additionally, it necessitates setting healthy boundaries and acquiring the ability to decline nonessential activities that divert our attention from our true priorities.

Intentionality: In today's fast-paced world, it's easy to let time, talent, and treasures slip through our fingers, void of purpose. But there is a way to reclaim control and turn your dreams into tangible realities! It all starts with intentionality. Intentionality is the power to actively choose how you allocate your resources, ensuring every moment counts. It's about making deliberate decisions and taking actions that align with your deepest values and aspirations in the kingdom. Like the law of motion, everything remains at rest until a relative force is applied.

Similarly, without intentional traction, your vision will stay a fantasy. By embracing intentionality, you unlock the pathway to converting your intangible dreams into tangible achievements. The secret ingredient propels you forward and transforms mere potential into concrete results. But remember, this transformation requires self-discipline and self-awareness. It demands making choices that contribute to your well-being and fuel your spiritual growth.

Balance: In pursuing kingdom success, it's essential to understand that God's purpose encompasses every aspect of your being: spirit, soul, and body. As we navigate the path of kingdom stewardship, seeking balance becomes paramount. A Bible passage that brings this into perspective is 3 John 2: "Beloved, I wish above all things that thou mayest prosper and be in health, even as thy soul prospereth." It becomes evident through the text that He desires prosperity and well-being for every dimension of your existence. As you ascend the ladder of success, it's crucial to allocate valuable time to nourish and cultivate growth in all areas, not just those deemed necessary. This entails avoiding extremes and discovering a healthy rhythm that allows you to fulfill your responsibilities, pursue your passions, nurture relationships, and find moments of rest and rejuvenation. Reflecting on the wisdom passed down to me by an elder statesman and Bishop; I learned the concept of avoiding being too tired, hungry, or angry. These insights serve as valuable reminders to prioritize self-care and maintain a balance as we journey toward our goals; a good example is how you are taking time to read this book.

CHAPTER

STEWARDSHIP CONNECTION TO TIME, TALENT, AND TREASURE

TIME, TALENT, AND Treasure are the three forms of currency we expend in our lives, which have the potential to impact our influence and our affluence. I will circle Time more comprehensively because it is uniquely positioned as the primary currency unit. Countless resources have been dedicated to discussing the concept of time management as the currency of life. What sets Time apart from money is that it cannot be saved or conserved like traditional forms of currency. It serves as the medium of exchange for developing our talents and acquiring treasures.

Time is a resource that encompasses both quality and quantity. When Moses prayed, "Teach us to number our days and recognize how few they are; help us to spend them as we should" **(Psalm 90:12,** Living Bible). Moses sought God's guidance in understanding how to add value in life with the Time he had on Earth. In retrospect, he is praying for wisdom in seizing the moment and wisely using God's opportunities.

In essence, encompassing the idea of quality and quantity in the conversation of using Time involves using the opportunities God presents us with as we strive to be good stewards. Quality is how we expend our moment on the Earth; quantity is cherishing the years we have spent and the right attitude of unlearning and learning new habits to enrich the times ahead that God will graciously render to us. The concept of quality lies in how we make the most of each precious moment bestowed upon us on this Earth. It's about investing our Time, energy, and resources in ways that bring value and purpose to our lives and the lives of others. Quality is the essence of living intentionally and making every second count.

On the other hand, quantity encompasses cherishing the years we have journeyed through and appreciating the experiences, lessons, and growth they have brought. It also involves the continuous process of unlearning and learning new habits that enrich our lives, preparing us for the abundant times that God, in His graciousness, will grant us in the future.

"The eloquent words of Carl F.H. Henry capture the essence of time as 'the divinely created sphere of God's preserving and redemptive work, and the arena of man's decision on his way to an eternal destiny' (p. 524). Reflecting upon this profound quote, we understand that God, in His infinite wisdom, has fashioned a framework known as Time. Within this framework, you and I are granted the remarkable opportunity to cultivate and nurture our talents and treasures, allowing them to blossom and reach their full potential.

To exist within the confines of Time itself is, in essence, an extraordinary gift bestowed upon us by God's grace. It is within the boundaries of Time that our dreams manifest into reality, intangible blessings are transformed into tangible manifestations, God's purposes are fulfilled, His love is tangibly felt and honored, and the Kingdom of God finds its true expression in shining glory.

In this divine dance of existence, Time becomes the canvas upon which we paint our lives, making choices and decisions that shape our eternal destiny. Through the prism of Time, we navigate the intricate tapestry of life, each moment an opportunity to align ourselves with God's will, experience His abundant grace, and contribute to the flourishing of His Kingdom on Earth.

Therefore, let us embrace Time's significance as a sacred gift from above. May we seize each fleeting second, recognizing that the potential for growth, transformation, and the realization of our divine calling lies within its grasp. As we journey through the boundless expanse of Time, let us do so with purpose, gratitude, and an unwavering commitment to living a life that reflects the glorious splendor of our Creator."

Time is a blessing of the LORD!

Isaiah 38: 18 NLT For the dead cannot praise you; they cannot raise their voices in praise. Those who go to the grave can no longer hope in your faithfulness. 19 Only the living can praise you as I do today. Each generation tells of your faithfulness to the next. 20 Think of it—the Lord is ready to heal me! I will sing his praises with instruments every day of my life in the Temple of the Lord.

CHAPTER

TIME
KINGDOM STEWARDSHIP OF TIME

> "Look carefully then how you walk, not as unwise but as wise, making the best use of the time, because the days are evil."
> —Ephesians 5:15-16

TIME, A PRECIOUS and limited resource entrusted to us by God, holds immense value in fulfilling our purpose and serving God and others. As stewards of Time, we are called to be intentional and wise in its use. This entails prioritizing our activities, aligning them with God's will and values, and making the "best" use of our Time, as the Scriptures advise.

As mentioned in the preceding chapter, it is crucial to remember that "Time is the canvas upon which we paint our lives, making choices and decisions that shape our eternal destiny." Therefore, determining our Time's "best use" becomes a profoundly personal journey, unique to each individual. In my personal experience, I have discovered immense joy in sketching illustrations while delivering lectures.

If we envision Time as a canvas, it is up to us to determine the size that aligns with our dreams. Just like an artist carefully selects colors, characteristics, and stroke styles to create their masterpiece, we too must make deliberate choices about how we want to utilize our Time on this Earth. This process necessitates introspection and discernment, allowing us to identify activities that resonate with God's will.

Examples of such activities are prayer, immersing ourselves in His Word, selflessly serving others, and cultivating relationships that foster spiritual growth. By engaging in these endeavors, we align ourselves with the divine plan, and our lives become a vibrant tapestry of purpose and fulfillment.

Conversely, we must be cautious of time-wasting activities that divert our attention and hinder our spiritual development. Distractions can impede our progress and prevent us from fulfilling God's calling. It is unwise to dedicate our lives to trivial matters, as the saying goes, "majoring in the minors."

As we continue our exploration, I will delve further into unique nature of time and vital ideas surrounding Time, building upon the initial references made at the beginning of this book. Time holds a paramount role as the framework within which we have the opportunity to showcase the magnificence of our talents and engage in the pursuit of our treasures. However, before we delve deeper into this topic, let us reflect upon the exercises presented below.

Consider the following practical exercises:

1. Reflect on Your Priorities: Reflect on your values and aspirations. Identify what truly matters to you and align your Time accordingly.

___

2. Create a Time Audit: Conduct a thorough assessment of how you currently spend your Time. Identify areas where adjustments can be made to align with your priorities.

___

3. Establish a Time Management System: Implement effective time management techniques, such as creating schedules, setting goals, and utilizing productivity tools to optimize your use of Time.

___

4. Seek Accountability: Find a trusted accountability partner or join a supportive community that can help you stay on track and hold you accountable for how you invest your Time.

___

5. Regular Evaluation and Adjustment: Continuously evaluate how you use your Time and make necessary adjustments to ensure alignment with your priorities and God's calling.

___

6. What adjustment can you start with today as a baby step to your greatness?

___

More Study materials

Genesis 6:3 The LORD said, "My Spirit will not put up with humans for such a long time, for they are only mortal flesh. In the future, their normal lifespan will be no more than 120 years." NLT

Psalm 90:10 The days of our years are threescore years and ten; and if because of strength they be fourscore years, yet is their strength labour and sorrow; for it is soon cut off, and we fly away. KJV

Ecclesiastes 3:1 KJV To everything there is a season, and a time to every purpose under the heaven:

THE UNIQUE NATURE OF TIME AS A CURRENCY OF LIFE

Time is a distinctive currency of life, emphasizing its finite and irreplaceable nature. Once Time is spent, it cannot be replenished or earned back. Each of us possesses a valuable resource, and how we invest and utilize, it shapes the outcomes and impact of our lives. Recognizing the unique nature of Time empowers us to prioritize our activities, make intentional choices, and use our Time in Earth wisely.

It is often said that we have no control over when, where, or how we are born, and we are uncertain about the Time of our passing. However, we are responsible for determining the quality of life we lead on Earth. Time is the trading factor available to us, placed at our disposal to manage and upgrade our situation. Yet, Time can also be elusive, as we perceive it through various lenses. One such perspective is the chronological lens, where individuals adopt a waiting attitude, counting the years and waiting for the opportune moment to take action. In addition to the "Chronos" concept, Scripture often references another notion called "kairos."

This perspective emphasizes that events and significant occurrences determine the timing and seasons of life rather than the reverse. When we encounter a kairos moment, it marks a pivotal time that shapes our journey. Just as in a road accident investigation, the question is asked, "At what time did this occur?"—the event becomes the catalyst for recording time and sets the stage for a season of investigation, research, and conviction.

Understanding the significance of kairos moments and the power of initiating a profitable season in our lives is crucial. It involves recognizing the divine opportunities, occurence, and appointed times that God presents to us. These moments hold the potential to unlock blessings, prosperity, and fulfillment in our lives and the lives of our families.

Your perspective on the uniqueness of Time will shape how you navigate these seasons and seize the opportunities they hold. By embracing the concept of kairos moments and developing a discerning mindset, we can make intentional choices and align ourselves with God's timing. Let us recognize that each season presents its opportunities and challenges, and our response to them determines the outcomes we experience. As we navigate life's journey, may we be attuned to the kairos moments, seize them with faith and courage, and embrace their transforming power?

Consider the following questions:

How do you actively initiate the prosperity God promised you and your family?

_____

_____

_____

What season are you in, and how can you leverage it effectively?

_____

_____

_____

_____

_____

When we grasp the distinctive essence of Time and its intrinsic connection to events, we can navigate life with purpose and intentionality. We realize that Time is not merely a fleeting commodity but a precious resource that requires our mindful investment. With this understanding, let us embark on a journey to unlock the full potential of this invaluable currency, making the most of every moment.

To make the most of Time, we must seize the opportunities that come our way. Recognizing that each encounter carries the potential for growth and transformation, we can approach life with open hearts and minds. By embracing new experiences, engaging in meaningful pursuits, and stepping out of our comfort zones, we create a tapestry of moments that enrich our lives and leave a lasting impact on those around us.

Scripture references:

Ephesians 5:15-16—"Look carefully then how you walk, not as unwise but as wise, making the best use of the time because the days are evil."

Psalm 90:12—"So teach us to number our days that we may get a heart of wisdom."

Explanation:

Ephesians 5:15-16: Reminds us to be wise in our lives, making the best use of our Time. It emphasizes the urgency and importance of using our Time wisely, considering the challenges and temptations of the world around us.

Psalm 90:12: Is a prayer of Moses, acknowledging the brevity of life and the need for wisdom in how we use our Time. It highlights the importance of seeking God's guidance and understanding in managing our Time effectively.

In our study of the unique nature of Time as a currency of life, we can explore the following discussion questions:

How do you currently view and prioritize your Time? Do you recognize its value and limited nature?

___

___

___

What are some everyday time-wasting activities or distractions in your life?

___

___

___

How can you overcome them to make better use of your Time?

___

___

___

How can we align our Time with God's purposes and prioritize activities that have eternal significance?

___

___

___

Are there any areas in your life where you feel you are misusing or neglecting your Time?

___

___

___

How can you make adjustments to ensure better stewardship of your Time?

_____

_____

_____

As we reflect on the unique nature of Time as a currency of life, let us strive to be intentional and wise in investing and spending this precious resource. May we seek God's guidance and wisdom in managing our Time effectively, aligning our priorities with His will, and living purposeful lives that bring glory to Him.

CHAPTER

THE LIMITED NATURE OF TIME

We must quickly carry out the tasks assigned to us by the one who sent us. The night is coming, and then no one can work.
—John 9:4

RECOGNIZING THE FINITE nature of Time and wisely utilizing it is of utmost importance. This understanding stems from the realization that our Time on Earth is limited and that our role in God's kingdom holds immense responsibility. It is crucial to acknowledge that God has entrusted us with a purpose beyond our comprehension. Consequently, every decision we make carries eternal consequences. Each passing day, hour, and moment is invaluable, and once Time slips away, it becomes irretrievable. We must harness the gift of Time to ensure we achieve the results we aspire to attain.

The challenge Time presents lies in its confinement to the present moment. While we may plan for the future or reflect upon the past, the truth remains that we can only navigate the realm of now. The book of Hebrews even highlights the significance of focusing on the present regarding our faith. "Now faith Is!" (Hebrews 11:1). Hence, it becomes vital for us to cherish and make the most of our 24/7 (Time), ensuring that we seize opportunities and fulfill our God-given purposes.

By recognizing the limited nature of Time and using it wisely, we demonstrate good stewardship and honor God with our lives.

Kingdom stewardship is Time-sensitive. His sovereigns can make one feel that God will always carry out His purpose, yet on the contrary, we may not be privileged with Time to accomplish his plan yet. Jesus refers to Time when you and I can no longer engage in Kingdom work. The gift and calling is without repentance, yet the gift's manifestation is more suitable. So God's plans and purpose can be limited by immobility in the human realm.

Let us seize the present moment, live intentionally, and seek to positively impact the Time we have been given. May we find wisdom in the Scriptures and the guidance of the Holy Spirit to help us make wise choices and prioritize our Time according to God's purposes.

Scripture:

Psalm 39:4-5 NLT "O Lord, make me know my end and what is the measure of my days; let me know how fleeting I am! Behold, you have made my days a few handbreadths, and my lifetime is as nothing before you. Surely all mankind stands as a mere breath!"

Poignantly expresses the fleeting nature of life. It highlights the reality that our days are short compared to eternity, urging us to gain a proper perspective on the limited nature of our Time on Earth.

James 4:14 NLT "Yet you do not know what tomorrow will bring. What is your life? For you are a mist that appears for a little time and then vanishes."

This Reminds us of the uncertainty and brevity of life. It underscores the fact that we do not have control over tomorrow and emphasizes the need to make the most of the Time we have been given.

The following conversation focuses on what I call a reality and mobility check. It requires introspection to unlearn and acquire new skills, embrace a fresh mindset, and cultivate the flexibility needed to adjust your path in your journey with God.

Discussion questions:

How does understanding life's brevity impact your priorities and choices?

_____
_____
_____
_____

Are there any areas in your life where you waste or mismanage your Time?

_____
_____
_____
_____

How can you improve in those areas?

_____

_____

_____

How can you balance the responsibilities and demands of life while ensuring that we use our Time wisely for God's purposes?

_____

_____

_____

What practical steps can you take to make the most of each day and invest your Time in activities that align with God's will?

_____

_____

_____

MOSES' PRAYER TO LEARN TO NUMBER OUR DAYS AND SPEND THEM WISELY

Psalm 90:12 KJV "So teach us to number our days that we may get a heart of wisdom."

Having unlearned or learned specific lessons in the previous exercise, we can confidently turn to Psalm 90 as a valuable resource for exploring prayer through the lens of kingdom stewardship. This particular prayer emphasizes the significance of being accountable for our days.

In Psalm 90:12, Moses implores us to "number our days" and utilize them wisely, highlighting the importance of seeking God's wisdom and guidance in managing our Time. This prayer serves as a plea to grasp the fleeting nature of life and cultivate a heart of wisdom that empowers us to maximize the precious days we have on this Earth.

Moses, the writer of Psalm 90, possessed a profound understanding of life's fleeting nature and the importance of recognizing the limitations of our Time. In verse 10 of the same psalm, he acknowledges that our years are relatively short, lasting around "seventy years, or even because of strength eighty." This serves as a poignant reminder of the brevity of our earthly existence. By praying to "number our days," Moses seeks God's assistance in comprehending each passing day's value and significance.

As stewards of God's kingdom, we easily overlook the significance of our assignments and fail to appreciate the spiritual growth opportunities presented by each day. It is uncanny how much content for spiritual growth one day delivers to your soul. Moses encourages us to become attentive learners in God's presence, recognizing that every day is filled with divine instructions and promptings from the Holy Spirit, which contain valuable insights necessary to fulfill God's purposes.

Take advantage of the opportunity to pick the gems on your journey. The true essence of effective kingdom stewardship lies in what we actively do and the revelations we may unintentionally disregard. Sometimes, we become so engrossed in our work that we overlook the hidden secrets God intends to reveal to maximize our productivity.

Practically speaking, numbering your days involves being attentive and prioritizing God's guidance regarding His assignment for your life. God's corrections are not based on our desires but are meant to align and direct us to His purpose and plans. It's comparable to modern cars equipped with road sensors that automatically correct your course and bring you back to the right lane when you veer off the road.

When God corrects us, particularly in areas that challenge our comfort zones, we may become irritable, uncomfortable, defensive, or aggressive. Our spirits resist the idea of change, so we miss out on the tremendous opportunity to indeed number our days.

It's crucial to remember that kingdom stewardship is God's plan, not ours. When we encounter correction, we should avoid taking it personally. Instead, we should embrace it as a necessary part of our journey. By surrendering to God's punishments and embracing change, we open ourselves to incredible growth and fulfillment of our God-given purpose.

Scripture references:

Psalm 119:105 Thy word is a lamp unto my feet and a light unto my path KJV

Matthew 6:33 But seek ye first the kingdom of God, and his righteousness; and all these things shall be added unto you. KJV

Matthew 6:34 Take therefore no thought for the morrow: for the morrow shall take thought for the things of itself. Sufficient unto the day is the evil thereof.

John 9:4 We must quickly carry out the tasks assigned us by the one who sent us. The night is coming, and then no one can work.

Colossians 4:5 "Live wisely among those who are not believers, and make the most of every opportunity. NLT

Discussion questions:

What does it mean to "number our days"? How does this perspective impact our understanding of Time?

_____
_____
_____
_____
_____
_____

Why is it important to seek a "heart of wisdom" in utilizing our Time? How does God's wisdom guide us in choosing how we spend our days?

_____
_____
_____
_____
_____
_____

How can we practically apply the concept of numbering our days in our daily lives? What changes should we make to ensure we use our Time wisely?

_____
_____
_____
_____
_____
_____

How does the awareness of the brevity of life shape our priorities, values, and goals?

_____
_____
_____
_____
_____
_____

How can we align them with God's purposes?

_____
_____
_____
_____
_____
_____

PART 2

CHAPTER

TALENTS
Discover | Develop | Deploy
KINGDOM STEWARDSHIP OF TALENT

"And Elisha said unto her, What shall I do for thee? Tell me, what hast thou in the house? And she said, Thine handmaid hath not anything in the house, save a pot of oil."
—2 Kings 4:2

TALENTS ARE THE unique abilities, skills, and gifts God has graciously given each individual. However, these talents are not meant to be kept hidden within ourselves. Instead, they are meant to be developed, nurtured, and utilized for God's glory and the betterment of others.

When we recognize that these talents are entrusted to us for a purpose, we begin to understand their potential to bring prosperity not only to ourselves but also to impact the lives of countless others. The extent to which our talents expand and grow depends on our willingness to embrace the process of continuous development.

In the story of the widow, we witness the transformative power of adjusting one's mindset and responding to the will of God. Her "oil," symbolizing the talents entrusted to us, flowed until there was no more room for further development. As stewards of our skills in God's Kingdom, we are called to discover and cultivate them and dream bigger, giving for God's favor to expand for more significant influence. These talents hold the key to releasing the goodness of God upon humanity.

To fully realize the potential of your talents, it requires investing time and effort into honing your skills at all levels. It involves using our abilities to foster personal growth, serving our immediate family, businesses, and Church families, and positively impacting our communities.

Moreover, we must actively seek opportunities to make a meaningful and lasting impact on the world around us. As you embark on this journey of talent development and impact, remember that your unique gifts have been entrusted to you by God. Embrace them, nurture them, and unleash them upon the world. In doing so, you not only fulfill your purpose but also contribute to the flourishing of others and ultimately bring glory to the One who bestowed these talents upon you.

Scripture: 1 Peter 4:10-11—"As each has received a gift, use it to serve one another, as good stewards of God's varied grace: whoever speaks, as one who speaks oracles of God; whoever serves, as one who serves by the strength that God supplies—so that in everything God may be glorified through Jesus Christ. To him belong glory and dominion forever and ever. Amen."

STEWARDSHIP OF TALENTS: DISCOVERY, DEVELOPMENT, AND DEPLOYMENT

Matthew 25:14 KJV "And unto one he gave five talents, to another two, and to another one; to every man according to his several ability; and straightway took his journey."

Stewardship of talents refers to the responsible management and use of the abilities and gifts God has bestowed upon us. It involves three key aspects: discovery, development, and deployment.

Discovery:

Recognizing and Understanding Our Talents

"The first crucial step in the stewardship of your talents is to uncover and embrace them fully. The concept of discovery emphasizes that your skills already exist within you, waiting to be acknowledged and utilized. There's no need to search further because every human has a unique set of talents essential for fulfilling their God-given purpose. It is only spiritual logic for God to equip one with the necessary gifts when He calls them for a specific assignment. These talents differ from the spiritual gifts commonly mentioned in scripture, although they, too, are divine gifts. Your talents encompass your natural inclinations, abilities, and tendencies, which are distinct to you and reflect God's intentional design. While the Bible describes various spiritual gifts, we will specifically focus on profiling the motivational skills mentioned in scripture, often called grace gifts.

In the parable of the talents found in Matthew 25:15, the Master distributed talents to his servants according to their "several abilities. These talents does not differ much from the spiritual gifts bestowed upon individuals when they become believers. These talents often become apparent during childhood and are the dispositions that the Bible encourages parents to nurture in their children, with the assurance that they will continue to manifest as they grow older (Proverbs 22:6 KJV "Train up a child in the way he should go: and when he is old, he will not depart from it.")

Within the New Testament text, these remarkable qualities and abilities are often referred to as motivational and grace gifts of the Spirit. While they may not be explicitly labeled as "talents," as we delve deeper into their essence, we come to realize that these gifts given by the Spirit of God align closely with the traits sought after by numerous corporate organizations, CEOs, and those seeking future employees, proteges, mentees, and collaborators.

These invaluable skills, talents, qualities, and abilities, made available through the grace of God, hold a profound significance. They are cherished within the realm of spirituality and highly sought after in secular domains. The same qualities that enhance the effectiveness and success of individuals within the Kingdom of God are often revered and desired by worldly entities.

As we embark on a journey to explore these divine gifts further, we begin to recognize their universal appeal. The attributes that propel individuals toward spiritual growth, impactful leadership, and fruitful collaboration are qualities that organizations and influential leaders seek in individuals who will contribute to their endeavors.

Therefore, as we uncover the depths of these motivational and grace gifts, we understand that they possess immense value beyond the confines of religious contexts. These gifts are transformative forces that shape our spiritual journeys and professional paths as they align with the qualities that organizations and visionary leaders recognize as essential for future growth and success.

Let us appreciate the interconnectedness of these Talents, gifts, and qualities, as they can elevate our spiritual walk and contributions within the secular realm. They are discussed in

Romans 12:3-8 and 1 Peter 4:10-11. They can be broadly categorized into speaking gifts and practical participation gifts (also known as serving or hands-on tendencies) (1 Peter 4:11).

_____

_____

_____

_____

Development:

Cultivating and Growing Our Talents

Once you have discovered your talents, the next crucial step is to develop them. It is not enough to identify your abilities; it requires willingness and effort to refine and enhance them. Talents are like raw materials—unpolished and in their initial form. Their actual value is realized when they are worked on and developed.

So, what does it take to develop your talents?

Take ownership of the direction of your life: Don't rely solely on other people's opinions. Let their feedback confirm what you already know God has spoken to you.

Stay focused on your inner motivation: By discovering your talents, adjust your life to make room for their use and expression.

Surround yourself with supportive people: Seek individuals who can help you develop your gifts further. If you don't have physical mentors, immerse yourself in books or resources that discuss your specific gifting.

Avoid the comparison trap: Each person's gifts come in different shades, colors, and intensities. Be content with what you have and use them to glorify God. Comparing yourself to others will only hinder your growth.

Let God position you for maximum impact: Don't push yourself or force opportunities. Instead, trust that God will place you in the correct positions and environments where you can effectively utilize your talents. Remember, the purpose of your gifts is to benefit others and bring glory to God.

The ultimate goal of being gifted is to bless others with your gifts. A gift that remains undiscovered cannot be developed, and a skill that is not developed cannot be fully utilized. God's ultimate purpose for your talents is to bring immeasurable blessings to those you encounter throughout your lifetime. You can begin using your gifting in every context of your relationships, whether within your family, Church, friendships, school, sports, entertainment, etc. Always remember that God has called and entrusted you with the stewardship of these gifts to bless humanity and bring fulfillment to your own life.

Scripture references:

Matthew 25:14-30 (Parable of the Talents): This parable illustrates the importance of utilizing and developing the talents entrusted to us by God.

Proverbs 18:16: "A gift opens the way and ushers the giver into the presence of the great."

Discussion Points:

Why is it important to actively develop and improve our talents instead of being complacent or neglecting them?

How can we balance humility and stewardship while pursuing the development of our talents? How can we ensure that our focus remains on serving God and others rather than seeking personal recognition?

Share practical strategies for developing talents, such as seeking mentorship, pursuing education or training, and engaging in consistent practice and improvement.

_____
_____
_____
_____
_____
_____
_____

Deployment:

Using Our Talents for God's Purposes

"In the context of 'deployment,' it denotes the purposeful execution of planned actions, translating theoretical concepts into practical applications to achieve specific outcomes or objectives. It marks the pivotal shift from mere planning to active implementation, bringing intended solutions or strategies to life.

Maintaining the proper perspective is paramount when harnessing your talents or gifts. It necessitates a serious and dedicated approach rather than treating them lightly or taking them for granted. While discovering one's gifting and skills is essential, having a clear action plan is equally crucial to avoid remaining in theory alone. God's divine plan is not theoretical; it calls us to action.

This perspective aims to instill a genuine and unwavering prayer life, where you actively seek God's guidance and remain vigilant for opportunities to utilize your gifts. It cultivates a humble mindset, acknowledging that using your skills glorifies God rather than seeking personal recognition or self-promotion."

To develop this perspective further, consider the following points:

Recognize the seriousness of your gifts: Understand that your talents and abilities are not to be taken lightly. "Your talents are divine blessings, bestowed upon you by God with a specific purpose in mind. They represent God's gift to you, meant to bring about transformation in your life and the world around you. Your talents are powerful tools for creating positive and godly changes in the universe. They are uniquely tailored to suit you and not intended for anyone else. Understanding the responsibility of stewardship is crucial to thriving with these gifts.

Within your talents lie the potential to solve future problems even before they arise. They are pregnant with revolutionary concepts and ideas that can transform how business is conducted. It is essential to carefully examine every thought related to using your talents, as they hold the potential to change lives profoundly." Someone said this a year ago, and I caught it; he said, "You are a blessing going somewhere to happen." Therefore, approach them with a sense of responsibility and gratitude.

Pray fervently and constantly: Being emotional means possessing a solid and intense passion, enthusiasm, or devotion towards something. In this case, that "something" is how to deploy your talent to create wealth for the Kingdom effectively. It signifies a deep and sincere commitment to a belief, cause, or goal. When someone is fervent in their kingdom stewardship, they demonstrate an unwavering dedication and zeal in pursuing God's interests or working towards God's objectives (Matthew 6:33).

Therefore, develop a habit of earnestly seeking God's guidance and revelation regarding the opportunities to use your gifts. Maintain an ongoing conversation with Him, asking for wisdom, discernment, and clarity in identifying the right avenues for service. You may start by volunteering your skill, finding areas that interest you, and serving there. Do not be concerned that sometimes some may want to abuse your gift. Tell yourself there is more from where that came from". You do this in prayer and remain hot to serve. Prayer is the key to staying alight with that passionate commitment to excellence for God. As you embrace your deployment, a daily consecration in prayer is non-negotiable.

Seek God's glory is not personal recognition: Align your heart with the desire to bring honor and glory to God through your talents. Avoid seeking personal acclaim or using your abilities for selfish purposes.

Instead, focus on how to magnify God's name and positively impact lives for the Kingdom.

Cultivate humility: Recognize that your talents are not a result of your efforts alone but are bestowed upon you by God's grace. Embrace humility as a virtue that allows you to serve others with a selfless and compassionate attitude. Let humility be the lens through which you approach using your gifts. (1 Corinthians 4:7 NLT) What gives you the right to make such a judgment? What do you have that God hasn't given you? And if everything you have is from God, why boast as though it were not a gift?)

Embrace God's timing and leading: Understand that God's timing is perfect, and He knows the best opportunities for you to use your gifts. Trust in His divine guidance and surrender control to Him. Be open to His leading and obedient to His direction, even if it means stepping out of your comfort zone or waiting for the right moment.

By developing this proper perspective, you will approach the use of your gifts with reverence, prayerfulness, and humility. This will enable you to align your actions with God's will and ultimately bring glory to His name through the impactful use of your gifts.

Scripture references:

1 Corinthians 12:4-7: "There are different kinds of gifts, but the same Spirit distributes them. There are different kinds of service, but the same Lord. There are different kinds of working, but in all of them and everyone, it is the same God at work. The manifestation of the Spirit is given to each one for the common good."

1 Peter 4:10-11: "Each of you should use whatever gift you have received to serve others, as faithful stewards of God's grace in its various forms. Anyone who speaks should do so with the understanding that

their words come from God. If anyone serves, they should do so with the strength God provides so that in all things, God may be praised through Jesus Christ. To him be the glory and the power forever and ever. Amen."

Discussion Points:

How does using your talents for God's purposes align with the principles of stewardship and the mission of the Church?

___

How can you actively deploy our talents within your church community and the broader society?

___

Share stories or examples of individuals who have effectively used their talents for God's purposes. What can you learn from their experiences?

___

Discuss potential obstacles or challenges hindering you from fully deploying your talents. How can you overcome these obstacles and cultivate a mindset of faithful stewardship?

_____
_____
_____
_____
_____
_____
_____
_____

By exploring the concepts of Discovery, Development, and Deployment of Talents in a biblical context, participants in the Bible study will gain a deeper understanding of their God-given gifts and their responsibility to steward them faithfully. This study will encourage individuals to reflect on their unique abilities, pursue growth and development, and actively use their talents for God's purposes, ultimately bringing glory to Him and making a difference in the world.

CHAPTER

MOTIVATION FOR DEPLOYING TALENTS
THROUGH LOVE—BY HUMILITY

THE PERSPECTIVE AND motivation for deploying our talents should be rooted in love, humility, and a desire to bless others. When we use our abilities with these qualities, we align ourselves with God's heart and purpose for our lives.

DEPLOY BY LOVE

1 Corinthians 13: 3 And though I bestow all my goods to feed people experiencing poverty, and though I give my body to be burned, and have not charity, it profiteth me nothing.

Love is the foundational pillar of our Christian faith, a profound force that propels the deployment of our unique talents. The significance of John 3:16 (16 "For this is how God loved the world: He gave[a] his one and only Son, so that everyone who believes in him will not perish but have eternal life) cannot be overstated, capturing the central purpose behind Jesus' mission in the world—a divine mission rooted in boundless love. In its purest form, this love becomes the catalyst for our service and benevolence towards others, reflecting the selflessness God has so graciously demonstrated to us.

It is this love that ignites the Spirit of stewardship within our hearts. As custodians of God's precious gifts, we recognize the responsibility entrusted to us, and love compels us to use these gifts wisely for the betterment of humanity. Unlike the Spirit of Hoarding, love lets us generously share our knowledge, opportunities, and resources with others, fostering mutual growth and support.

Through our love for God and our fellow beings, we discover the profound meaning behind our service to humanity. In these acts of love-driven kindness, we find purpose and fulfillment. Love keeps us steadfast in selfless dedication, ensuring our actions remain guided by compassion and empathy.

With profound devotion to the love of God and an unwavering love for people's destinies, we embark on a journey of love-infused stewardship. Love opens our hearts to the needs of others, enabling us to touch lives positively and make a genuine difference in this world.

Ultimately, living in the light of love and stewarding our gifts with care allow us to live out the core tenets of our Christian faith. By embracing love and serving with compassion, we become vessels of hope, radiating God's love to a world that yearns for kindness and unity."

DEPLOY WITH HUMILITY

Humility holds a central place in acknowledging that our talents are divine gifts bestowed upon us by God rather than something to boast about or take credit for. It serves as an essential anchor, grounding us and reminding us that our abilities are meant to be used for the greater good and to advance God's Kingdom. Just as one cannot climb a ladder from the top, actual promotion within the Kingdom necessitates humility. Serving from a position of humility is far more impactful than attempting to do it from a place of authority.

Remarkably, when individuals reach the pinnacle of success through service, their scope of service tends to expand even further. Humility propels them to seek out more ways to serve others selflessly. Rising to the top is not about attaining a position of authority but becoming a better servant.

Talent without humility will lead to eventual humiliation. Desiring greatness must be coupled with a heart of servitude. Humility ignites the Spirit of stewardship, enabling us to perceive unique needs that arrogance could never discern. It is akin to a flashlight in the darkness, illuminating areas that require our attention and care.

In the footsteps of Christ, we are encouraged to adopt a lowly mind—a mind characterized by humility. Just as a stamp is indispensable for sending a parcel, humility becomes the seal that renders the deployment of our gifts worthy and effective. In our modern context, just as an email requires a functioning email address for successful delivery, our facilities must be imbued with humility to make a meaningful impact.

Thus, humility is an indispensable virtue, guiding us in the responsible and compassionate deployment of our God-given talents. It serves as a reminder that these gifts are not about self-glorification but rather about uplifting and helping others for the greater purpose of God's Kingdom.

Scripture references:

1 Corinthians 13:1-3: This passage highlights the importance of love in all aspects of our lives, including the use of our talents. Without love, our actions are empty and meaningless.

Philippians 2:3-4: Paul encourages believers to be humble, considering others more significant than themselves. This mindset fosters a selfless approach to deploying our talents

1 Peter 4:10-11: Peter reminds believers that our gifts are given to serve others, and we should do so with the strength and grace that God provides.

Bible Study Discussion Points:

Reflect on the role of love in deploying our talents. How do love for God and others shape our perspective and actions when using our gifts?

_____
_____
_____
_____

Discuss the significance of humility in the context of talent deployment. How does humility guard against pride and selfishness in utilizing our abilities?

_____

_____

_____

_____

Reflect on personal experiences of deploying talents. How have love, humility, and the desire to bless others influenced the impact and outcomes of your service

_____

_____

_____

_____

Discussion Questions:

1. Discovering and Identifying Your God-Given Talents.
    a. What steps can we take to explore and uncover our unique talents?

    _____

    _____

    _____

    b. How can self-reflection, introspection, and seeking guidance help us in this process?

    _____

    _____

    _____

c. Are there any practical exercises or assessments that can assist in identifying our God-given talents?

_____
_____
_____
_____

2. Developing and Nurturing Your Talents
   a. What are some effective strategies for developing and honing our talents?

   _____
   _____
   _____
   _____

   b. How can we seek opportunities for growth and improvement in our specific areas of talent?

   _____
   _____
   _____
   _____

   c. Are there any mentors, coaches, or resources that can help us nurture and expand our abilities?

   _____
   _____
   _____
   _____

3. Utilizing Your Talents for Service and God's Glory
   a. How can our talents be utilized to serve others and make a positive impact?

   _____
   _____
   _____
   _____

   b. How can we align our talents with the values and teachings of God to bring glory to His name?

   _____
   _____
   _____
   _____

   c. Are there any examples or stories demonstrating the power of using talents for God's Kingdom?

   _____
   _____
   _____
   _____

4. Identifying Areas of Significant Impact
   a. Reflecting on your unique talents, what specific areas of service or ministry resonate with you the most?

   _____
   _____
   _____
   _____

b. How can you leverage your talents to make a significant difference?

_____
_____
_____
_____

c. Are there any practical steps you can take to explore and pursue opportunities in those specific areas? More scripture to consider:

_____
_____
_____
_____

Scripture references:

Exodus 4:2 "And the LORD said unto him, What is that in thine hand? And he said, A rod."

Exodus 4:21 "And the LORD said unto Moses, When thou goest to return into Egypt, see that thou do all those wonders before Pharaoh, which I have put in thine hand: but I will harden his heart, that he shall not let the people go."

Luke 8:16 "No man, when he hath lighted a candle, covereth it with a vessel, or putteth it under a bed; but setteth it on a candlestick, that they which enter in may see the light."

Matthew 13:46 "Who, when he had found one pearl of great price, went and sold all that he had, and bought it."

CHAPTER

UNDERSTANDING GRACE GIFTS

Romans 12: 6 In his grace, God has given us different gifts for doing certain things well. So if God has given you the ability to prophesy, speak out with as much faith as God has given you.

7 If your gift is serving others, serve them well. If you are a teacher, teach well.

8 If your gift is to encourage others, be encouraging. If it is giving, give generously. If God has given you leadership

ability, take the responsibility seriously. And if you have a gift for showing kindness to others, do it gladly.

DRAWING INSPIRATION FROM the Scripture Ephesians 4:11-12, we can look into the array of the fivefold ministry gifts God bestowed upon the church's body. Over the years, the church has placed significant emphasis and extensive teachings on what is commonly known as the five-fold ministry gifts, which Jesus imparted to the body. As revealed in the Scripture, these gifts aim to equip the saints for their ministry work. Termed ascension gifts, their stewardship involves training and preparing the rest of the body to discover, develop, and utilize (deploy) their talents, which is crucial for fulfilling God's redemption plan.

In this book, my chosen approach is to explore how these gifts and talents can facilitate through their diverse expression in various aspects to equip the saints life, to harness and perfect their service, particularly in the marketplace, business innovations, creativity, networks, and other general endeavors that advance the Kingdom of God. Let us delve into the first, prophesy

PROPHESY

The gift of perceiving the future. Individuals endowed with this gift possess a heightened ability to discern and perceive how future events align with God's plans. They are the mouthpiece of God that expresses God's desires and plan for the body of Christ.

They are granted the grace to anticipate and position themselves, their organizations, churches, and even the entire body of Christ at large for optimal utilization of the glorious opportunities presented by God.

Jesus referred to this as knowledge of "things" that will take place (John 16:13).

This gift can be likened to being a futurist because they are God's futurist as it empowers the recipient to accurately predict future events with an outstanding strategy for effective implementation of divine instruction. (Hosea 12;13 NLT. Then by a prophet, the LORD brought Jacob's descendants out of Egypt, and by that prophet, they were protected). (Mark 9:30–32; Acts 11:28; 2 Timothy 3:1).

Although outside of the Kingdom, individuals with this gift would be called futurists. They specialize in studying and predicting future trends, developments, and possibilities across various fields and disciplines. These futurists engage in foresight activities, analyzing current data, technological advancements, social changes, and other relevant factors to make informed projections about what lies ahead.

They can be found in academia, consulting firms, think tanks, research organizations, and corporate settings. This gift is not only instrumental in guiding the body of Christ, which is the traditional understanding, but it can govern and right predict world strategies as they unfold. This paradigm is still a virgin experience in the body, but it is slowly being embraced that the gift is paving the way in the so call "secular" space.

However, when it comes to stewardship of this talent within the Kingdom, believers with the gift of prophecy have the advantage of operating in all the above spaced and higher on a supernatural level. The presence of the Holy Spirit elevates their awareness of the future. Jesus reiterated multiple times in the New Testament that believers would know things to come, walking in the light rather than darkness.

They are likened to a city on a hill, shining brightly and leading the way (Matthew 5:14). In the book of Deuteronomy; God promised His children that they would be the head and not the tail, positioned ahead of the world in terms of leadership and insight.

Therefore, those with the gift of prophecy possess a unique ability to navigate the future guided by the Spirit, surpassing even their secular counterparts. It takes this spiritual awareness to a whole new dimension. By embracing and utilizing this gift, believers can tap into divine wisdom and discernment, enabling them to lead effectively and profoundly impact the world around them.

GIFT of SERVICE

Romans 12:7 Or ministry, let us wait on our ministering: or he that teacheth, on teaching;

The term "ministry" has its roots in the Greek word "diakonia" (διακονία), encompassing the concepts of ministry, ministration, and serving.

While some associate it primarily with the role of a deacon in a church setting, its initial translation reveals a broader meaning: to be in service and carry out the commands of others. However, it is essential to note that being in service does not imply a slave-master relationship, for, in truth, we are all servants of God. Even those in positions of authority are ultimately servants of God.

Understanding this mindset is crucial when operating in the gift of service, as it allows us to fulfill our duties effectively to God's glory. Embracing servanthood is God's call for effective stewardship, and greatness is achieved through service. As Jesus said, the path to greatness is through serving others.

This definition of service applies to any context where assistance is required, regardless of the capacity. Whenever we witness greatness, it often reflects a history of exceptional service. Excellence emerges from fervently serving at high levels with the gifts or talents bestowed upon us.

The third aspect of the translation of "Diakonia" relates to rendering Christian affection through ministration, particularly in helping others by collecting or distributing charities. It is essential not to confine this expression of service solely to brethren within the church, as the talent for service extends to various spheres.

The central theme of this book undoubtedly revolves around service, which is also exemplified through other terms in Scripture, such as being a servant, minister, or steward. The Greek word for "servant" is "oikononomos," sharing its root with "economy," implying the role of a household manager. This understanding highlights the humble authority and usefulness inherent in those gifted with such a calling.

Throughout Scripture, the success or failure of characters is often measured by the quality of their service, categorizing them as either faithful or unfaithful servants. Hebrews 3:5 (NIV) emphasizes Moses' faithfulness as a servant in God's house, bearing witness to what God would speak in the future.

In the New Testament, believers are blessed with a significant privilege: receiving God's Spirit of service, empowering them to embrace a deeper level of servanthood or stewardship. As this understanding grows, the marketplace can be governed by kingdom citizens who embody the heart of a servant to a greater extent.

Below, we can explore the vast scope where the gift of service can be unleashed in service to the Kingdom of God. Examples of service industry sectors include:

Hospitality and Tourism: This includes hotels, restaurants, travel agencies, tour operators, resorts, and other related services catering to travelers and tourists.

Financial Services: Banks, insurance companies, investment firms, credit card companies, and other financial institutions fall under this category.

Healthcare and Wellness: Hospitals, clinics, doctors, nurses, therapists, fitness centers, spas, and other healthcare and wellness providers are part of this sector.

Professional Services: This encompasses various professional fields, including legal services, accounting, consulting, advertising, architecture, engineering, and information technology

Retail and Wholesale Trade: The service industry also includes businesses involved in the buying and selling goods, such as retailers, wholesalers, and e-commerce platforms.

Transportation and Logistics: Airlines, shipping companies, courier services, freight operators, and logistics providers are integral to this sector.

Entertainment and Media: Movie theaters, broadcasters, streaming platforms, music studios, publishing houses, and other entertainment and media-related services fall into this category.

Discussion

What area or sectors are your talent found?

_____
_____
_____
_____
_____
_____
_____

GIFT of TEACHER

Teacher: Armed with the quest or thirst for knowledge and revelation to hold meaningful discourse and life-changing conversations with others to instruct them with the wisdom of God. The command in the great commission stipulates as a church; we should go and teach all nations.

The word nation is translated from the Greek word "ethnos," where were derive the word ethnic. In this context, Jesus' command is not just winning souls and teaching about baptisms and discipline in a church context. Instead, when Jesus gave this command, there were no churches as we have today; instead, there were communities of people who engaged in all works of life.

Jesus' command fell on the ears of men who did not have our modern church concept, so how would they teach all ethnos concerning things of the Kingdom without supernatural insights, strategies, and directives that will be expressed through the gift of teaching? He commanded teaching them to observe all things that I have commanded you, and lo, I am with you always, even to the end of the age." Amen.

Furthermore, while we look at the present ecclesiastical structure to understand these gifts, we may need help understanding their expressions because the system when it was given was different from what we have now. Therefore, if we have access to faithful kingdom stewardship and the impact God intends for the church to possess.

Here is Jesus deploying His disciple to go into the world to teach the world what He has taught them over three intensive years with the master.

In order the fully grasp the power of this teaching gift, the choice of words here matters; let us pause to emphasize that the teaching gift in this Scripture is not the same as we read earlier in **Ephesian 4: 18-19**;

although it may carry the few elements, the express is different, The latter is a headship life of Jesus. But the subject here is the gift of grace in the body to bring about the truth of God's wisdom to impact society at large.

Here are some space that anointed and gifted teachers can impact lives for the kingdom

Educational Institutions: From elementary schools to universities, individuals with the gift of teaching are instrumental in conveying knowledge and skills to students. They cultivate conducive learning environments and simplify intricate concepts for effective understanding.

Corporate Training: Within businesses and organizations, those possessing the gift of teaching are crucial for conducting training sessions. They adeptly communicate information, company policies, and procedural guidelines to ensure employee comprehension.

Professional Advancement: The gift of teaching is vital for delivering ongoing training and development initiatives, enabling employees to refine their skills and stay abreast of industry trends.

Technical Sectors: In specialized fields such as IT, engineering, and healthcare, individuals with the gift of teaching can demystify complex subjects for diverse audiences.

Sales and Marketing: The gift of teaching is advantageous for training sales teams on product knowledge, persuasive communication, and effective customer engagement strategies.

Healthcare and Medical Training: Medical professionals with the gift of teaching contribute by instructing students, interns, and residents, sharing practical experience and knowledge.

Public Speaking and Workshops: Those endowed with the gift of teaching can engage audiences through public speaking and seminar leadership, conveying information across a spectrum of subjects.

Nonprofits and Community Initiatives: In educational nonprofits and community organizations, teachers are indispensable for fostering learning, skill development, and personal growth.

Parenting and Family Programs: Individuals with the gift of teaching play a role in guiding parents and caregivers in effective child-rearing and family dynamics through workshops and educational programs.

Spiritual and Religious Guidance: The gift of teaching is paramount for religious leaders imparting wisdom, faith, and moral values to their congregations.

Content Creation: Individuals with the gift of teaching can craft educational materials, online courses, and written content to enlighten and educate readers.

Language Instruction: The teaching gift is invaluable when instructing non-native speakers in learning languages, requiring patience, clear communication, and adept breakdown of intricate concepts.

Life Coaching and Personal Development: Those with the gift of teaching serve as life coaches, aiding individuals in setting goals, conquering challenges, and experiencing personal growth.

Artistic and Creative Fields: In artistic disciplines like music, dance, and fine arts, individuals with the gift of teaching nurture creativity and technical proficiency in students.

Across these diverse arenas, individuals possessing the gift of teaching wield the power to communicate, inspire, and guide others toward their zenith of personal and professional achievement. They cultivate learning experiences that empower individuals to fulfill their potential.

_____
_____
_____

Gifts of the Exhorter:

Apollos, a remarkable individual, embodies a unique set of qualities within the body of Christ. He is an encourager, optimist, motivator, and a catalyst for courage in others. This extraordinary gift he possesses lifts the entire body of Christ, empowering them to lead fulfilling lives. One of the ways this gift manifests is through his eloquence and ability to articulate thoughts effectively.

In the Bible, Apollos is a prime example of someone who truly epitomizes this exceptional gift. He was a 1st-century Alexandrian Jewish Christian, mentioned multiple times in the New Testament. Being a contemporary and colleague of Paul the Apostle, Apollos played a crucial role in the early establishment and growth of the churches in Ephesus and Corinth.

In Acts 18:24, we learn that Apollos, a knowledgeable and eloquent speaker well-versed in the Scriptures, arrived in Ephesus from Alexandria, Egypt. His presence undoubtedly left a lasting impact on the community, inspiring and uplifting the believers in their faith journey.

Encouragement comes from the Old French word encourager, meaning "make strong, hearten." It denotes the same meaning as the Hebrew text. Where exhorters are, there is always Strength and courage to make impossible tasks possible. God gave this gift and Strength to individuals who will become ministers in complex and challenging professions.

There is an "ethnos" that God wants to bring witness to for effectiveness and redemption.

It is evident that when looking at history, I will list below have they're with Christian people that believe God called them to found such:

Missionaries: Christian missionaries often travel to remote and challenging regions to spread their faith and provide humanitarian aid.

Chaplains: Christian chaplains serve in various settings, including hospitals, the military, and prisons, offering spiritual support and guidance to those in need.

Humanitarian Aid Workers: Christians involved in humanitarian organizations work in conflict zones and disaster-stricken areas, providing essential aid and relief to affected communities.

Nonprofit Founders: Christians who start nonprofits to address social issues or assist vulnerable populations display courage in advocating for change and leading their organizations.

Pastors and Religious Leaders: Leading a congregation and guiding others spiritually requires courage, empathy, and dedication.

Christian Counselors: These professionals provide emotional and psychological support to individuals facing various challenges in life.

Christian Activists: Advocating for social justice and standing up for marginalized communities often involves facing opposition and personal risk.

Foster and Adoptive Parents: Christians who open their homes and hearts to foster or adoptive children demonstrate courage in providing loving homes and stability to those in need.

Christian Educators: Teachers who incorporate their faith into their teaching and create a safe, nurturing environment for their students exhibit courage and commitment to their values.

Christian Doctors and Nurses: Healthcare professionals who integrate their faith into their practice and care for patients with compassion and empathy display courage and dedication.

Christian Lawyers: Advocating for justice and defending the rights of others requires bravery and a commitment to upholding moral principles.

Christian Artists and Writers: Creators who use their talents to address challenging issues, inspire others, and promote positive messages demonstrate courage through art.

_____
_____
_____
_____
_____
_____
_____

GIFT of GIVERS
"If it is giving, then give generously."

The gift of giving may initially be perceived as making one frivolous and easily parting with what they have. However, this remarkable gift is bestowed upon individuals with a strong desire to support and finance God's work on Earth.

They possess a profound discipline that enables them to exercise delayed gratification, being attuned to God's guidance in spending matters. Those gifted with giving can generate substantial resources and wealth because of their generous hearts dedicated to the Kingdom of God. Their driving force is to channel resources into advancing God's mission. For them, Matthew 6:33 may become a personal mantra—a guiding principle for their lives.

These individuals may face life lessons that demand resilience beyond the ordinary throughout their journey. God might take them through unique challenges, strengthening their character and devotion. Through this gift, revival is sustained, as they play a vital role in supporting and uplifting God's work. It is through Barnabas (son of and His Gift of Giving that the early Church rose to sustain the move of God. Acts 4:36 KJV And Joses, who by the apostles was surnamed Barnabas, (which is, being interpreted, The son of consolation,) a Levite, and of the country of Cyprus.

In the remarkable early days of the Church, amidst the divine addition of those to be saved, a figure shone brightly—an exceptional man named Barnabas. He stood as a profound embodiment of those gifted with the unparalleled ability to give, going beyond the ordinary to bless others with generosity that defied expectations. This gift birthed an entirely new ministry that beautifully complemented and sustained the exponential growth of God's Kingdom.

Matthew 7:6 KJV: "Give not that which is holy unto the dogs, neither cast ye your pearls before swine, lest they trample them under their feet and turn again and rend you."

Amidst the brilliance of the gift of giving, some encountered bewilderment as they were often perceived as being frugal or tight-fisted. This enigma compelled me to earnest prayer, seeking to comprehend why those who yearned to give selflessly found themselves misunderstood.

And in this quest for understanding, the secret hidden within the verse above emerged, though it may initially sound condescending. The truth unveiled is that this unique gift holds the profound responsibility of safeguarding and allocating the wealth it generates solely according to God's divine directives.

The reality is that not all needs will captivate the heart of a giver to address. Some may be distractions or unworthy of consuming the precious resources of God's Kingdom. Those endowed with the gift of giving possess an acute awareness that the wealth they have acquired is not a product of their prowess, intelligence, or ingenuity. They firmly acknowledge that God, in His wisdom, will direct them to where these resources are most needed.

Givers need to be diligently trained in attuning their ears to the voice of God, particularly during seasons of abundant favor and unprecedented prosperity in their businesses. At these times, the temptation to exceed God's direction and engage in misguided generosity may arise. It is not enough to give merely because one has the means; true giving stems from the divine prompting of God's guiding hand.

2 Corinthians 9:10-11 KJV: "Now he that ministereth seed to the sower both minister bread for your food, and multiply your seed sown, and increase the fruits of your righteousness; Being enriched in everything to all bountifulness, which causeth through us thanksgiving to God."

Remarkably, givers embrace a profound realm—they are sowers. God strategically ministers seeds to these sowers; individuals are chosen by divine wisdom to yield the most extraordinary results. Here, the "best result" entails not just the growth and maturation of the seed but also the impeccable dispensation of the ensuing harvest. God and Givers do not sow their seeds haphazardly during the planting season; instead, they carefully entrust their sources of visions, ideas, strategies for increase, dreams of the night, and even prophetic words to experienced spiritual farmers.

These individuals have well-maintained farmlands, where each seed can receive maximum care, leading to an unparalleled harvest. God is portrayed as the ultimate Farmer (husbandman) in John 15:1-2, who will return to gather His bountiful harvest. Givers cover this sacred realm, as God has entrusted them with the profound ability to increase and multiply His divine provisions.

GIFT OF RULER
Administrator, organiser, management tendency.

Romans 12:8 KJV Or he that exhorteth, on exhortation: he that giveth, let him do it with simplicity; **he that ruleth,** with diligence; he that showeth mercy, with cheerfulness.

The Greek word used in the reference is "proistemi," it is different in usage from the phrase megas, where Jesus was asked by His disciples Who shall be "megas" among them? In other words, who shall be influential and lead in great power? Then Jesus answered them with these words, "Let him be your minister.

(Matthew 20:26 NLT "But among you, it will be different. Whoever wants to be a leader among you must be your servant.")

In Roman 12 8, The word proistemi uses connoting one who organizes, an administrator, and one whose innate capacity is to bring solutions to complex situations and are invaluable to organizations. To rule is to get the order in a practical and fun way. Proistemi also refers to a superintendent, or one who presides over projects, people at work, or Church, as it were.

This gift gives individuals the extraordinary power to revolutionize organizations with unparalleled administrative prowess, elevating their service to the highest levels of excellence. The spirit of excellence is a rare and precious attribute, a divine manifestation fueled by the presence of the Holy Spirit. Wherever the Holy Spirit abides, order and excellence flourish, rising to the highest levels of manifestation.

Those who embrace this spirit exude a profound sense of self-worth, unafraid to showcase their immeasurable value to the organization. Their aura of excellence demands attention and refuses to be ignored, setting them apart as exceptional leaders. Through this gift, they govern with mastery, using excellence as their guiding compass to chart a course of success.

In the tapestry of biblical characters, one name emerges as the epitome of the spirit of excellence: Daniel. Daniel was favored above all others in the realm; his rise was attributed to the extraordinary spirit dwelling within him—the heart of excellence.

(Daniel 6:3 KJV; Then this Daniel was preferred above the presidents and princes because an excellent spirit was in him, and the king thought to set him over the whole realm) Even the queen of King Belshazzar bore witness to Daniel's exceptional disposition, praising him for possessing a spirit of wisdom and understanding akin to that of the gods.

Daniel's keen awareness of his gift empowered him to wield it faithfully as a steward, serving four kings throughout his lifetime, including Belshazzar.

Daniel 5:11 KJV; Then was king Belshazzar greatly troubled, and his countenance was changed, and his lords were astonished. Then King Belshazzar was greatly troubled, and his face was changed, and his lords were astonished. There is a man in thy kingdom, in whom is the spirit of the holy gods; and in the days of thy father light and understanding and wisdom, like the wisdom of the gods, was found in him; whom the king Nebuchadnezzar thy father, the king, I say, thy father, made master of the magicians, astrologers, Chaldeans, and soothsayers; the essence of the ruler's gift lies in wisdom and the ability to navigate challenging situations with unparalleled wit. While possessing this gift is not a prerequisite for occupying high positions like a CEO or a lead pastor, its presence becomes an invaluable asset when needed. Daniel 2:22 NLT He reveals deep and mysterious things and knows what lies hidden in darkness, though he is surrounded by light.

As with all gifts, the process of discovery and maturation is paramount. As great organizers, rulers must undergo proper processing and training before deployment. Joseph, another biblical character, demonstrated an exceptional gift to the ruler from a young age.

Genesis 37:2 KJV "These are the generations of Jacob. Joseph, being seventeen years old, was feeding the flock with his brethren; and the lad was with the sons of Bilhah, and with the sons of Zilpah, his father's wives: and Joseph brought unto his father their evil report."

His dreams of ruling in the future over his family incited envy and nearly led to tragedy. However, through God's providence, Joseph's ruling gift later played a pivotal role in sustaining the Egyptian economy, making Egypt a world economic powerhouse.

Yet, the temptation to operate this gift prematurely can be difficult. Joseph's initial naivety nearly jeopardized his destiny, but through growth and maturation, he harnessed his skill effectively. The talent to "ruler "must be carefully nurtured and cultivated, only to be deployed at the right Time, ensuring its full potential is realized. Thus, embracing and mastering this gift of rulership becomes a transformative journey of becoming an exceptional leader, charting a course of excellence and success in the pursuit of divine purpose.

Proverbs 17:27: Knowledge and understanding are two close words that explain the manifestation of the spirit of excellence. The spirit of excellence can only operate where the Holy Spirit resides.

Below are few contexts, individuals with the gift of administration excel at organizing, coordinating, and leading teams and resources to achieve objectives efficiently and effectively. Their skills contribute to the overall success and smooth functioning of various industries and organizations.

Business Management: Administrators play a crucial role in managing businesses, overseeing operations, coordinating teams, and ensuring efficient workflow.

Project Management: The gift of administration is essential in planning, organizing, and executing projects. Administrators ensure that projects are completed on time, within budget, and meet the desired outcomes.

Event Planning: Administrators excel in coordinating events, conferences, and seminars. They manage logistics, schedules, and details to ensure the smooth execution of gatherings.

Nonprofit Organizations: The gift of administration is vital in nonprofit organizations, where administrators manage resources, budgets, and programs to achieve the organization's mission.

Church Leadership: Administrators in churches oversee various aspects, including

Government and Public Services: The gift of administration is valuable in government agencies, where administrators handle policy implementation, program management, and public services.

Human Resources: Administrators in HR manage employee records, benefits, recruitment, and ensure compliance with labor laws.

Financial Management: Administrators in finance oversee budgets, financial planning, and ensure proper allocation of resources.

Real Estate Management: In real estate, administrators handle property management, leasing, and tenant relations.

GIFT OF MERCY
Psalms 103:8 KJV The Lord is merciful and gracious, slow to anger, and plenteous in mercy.

If you would love a favorite, this will be it. It is the hallmark of God the Father. It is as though God the Father a vital piece of who he is and dispenses to some. Mercy is an enviable ability that some can only display to the extent it makes most of us hardhearted; They are God's angels on the Earth in human coats. Where will the world be with the mercy givers? The one who feels deeply that the usual humanity.

Another note is that the Apostle Paul mentions them last on the list. However, on closer scrutiny, you will find that in all gifts, various levels of mercy are needed for them to be fully functional. Mercy is a compassionate and benevolent quality that is required in multiple aspects of life and work.

You're discussing the significance and power of the gift of mercy in various aspects of life, particularly in leadership, teaching, giving, and encouraging others. Your points show that understanding and embracing mercy can bring positive impacts and foster a compassionate environment.

Indeed, the gift of prophecy or leadership can sometimes be misunderstood, and having mercy helps the individual handle such situations with compassion and understanding. A faithful servant or leader who carries out their duties with mercy can profoundly influence those they lead, creating a more supportive and empathetic atmosphere.

For teachers, mercy helps them remain patient and humble, primarily when the desired results don't immediately manifest in their students. Similarly, exhorters who operate with a higher level of mercy can effectively encourage and support others.

The giver with mercy avoids the pitfalls of appearing greedy, and instead, they can make a positive impact by helping those in need. The guidance of mercy may lead them to assist organizations or individuals they might not initially consider deserving. Still, such acts can have a transformative impact on both the giver and the recipient.

Compassion is crucial for rulers and leaders as it makes them more understanding and benevolent. Without mercy, those in positions of power may become harsh and controlling, leading to a hostile work environment.

However, it's also essential to strike a balance, as excessive mercy may lead to feeling overwhelmed by the emotions of others and a sense of helplessness. Hence, cheerfulness and a firm understanding of boundaries can make this gift more effective.

Incorporating mercy into work settings, as you mentioned, indeed promotes empathy, understanding, and resilience among employees. A compassionate work environment fosters teamwork, productivity, and overall well-being, benefiting individuals and the organization.

The gift of mercy is powerful and, when utilized with wisdom, can positively impact various realms of life, leading to a more compassionate and harmonious society.

In Summary, these gifts can manifest in various ways, and each individual's unique disposition and talents are part of their distinctive contribution to society. Some individuals may have edges or gifts that are remarkably distinct, setting them apart from others in their abilities.

These unique giftings can be on a personal level, within families, organizations, or even entire countries.

These gifts serve a specific purpose and contribute to the broader tapestry of human experience and interactions.

Recognizing, embracing, and utilizing these gifts effectively can lead to transformative impacts in various areas of life. The diversity of talents and giftings allows for a more comprehensive approach to addressing challenges and meeting the needs of individuals and communities.

Believers need to discern and develop their unique giftings and use them in ways that align with their values, faith, and calling. By doing so, they can play an active role in making the world a better place and advancing the purposes of God in their spheres of influence. Furthermore, recognizing and appreciating the diverse gifts in others can lead to a more harmonious and collaborative society.

Below are some areas where gift of mercy is crucial:

Interpersonal Relationships: In workplaces and organizations, showing mercy to colleagues and team members can foster a supportive and understanding environment. Offering forgiveness for mistakes or misunderstandings can promote healthy relationships and improve teamwork.

Leadership and Management: Leaders who lead with mercy tend to inspire loyalty and trust in their teams. Granting second chances, providing constructive feedback with kindness, and considering the well-being of employees are all ways mercy can positively impact leadership.

Disciplinary Actions: When addressing workplace issues or disciplinary matters, a merciful approach can allow for fairness and understanding. Balancing consequences with compassion can help individuals learn from their mistakes and grow professionally.

Customer Service: In customer-facing roles, practicing mercy can lead to better outcomes when handling challenging situations. Responding with empathy and understanding to customers' concerns can enhance their overall experience and build brand loyalty.

Community and Social Responsibility: Extending mercy to those in need and supporting charitable initiatives can have a positive impact on society and demonstrate a commitment to social responsibility

Discussion Points:

How does recognizing and embracing our God-given talents contribute to our overall sense of purpose and fulfillment?

_____
_____
_____
_____

What are some practical ways we can discover and identify our talents? How can self-reflection, seeking counsel, and exploring various areas of service help in this process?

_____
_____
_____
_____

Share personal experiences of discovering and acknowledging your talents. How did this impact your understanding of God's design for your life?

PART 3

CHAPTER

STEWARDSHIP OF TREASURE

"Do not lay up for yourselves treasures on Earth, where moth
and rust destroy and where thieves break in and steal, but
lay up for yourselves treasures in heaven, where neither moth
nor rust destroys and where thieves do not break in and steal.
For where your treasure is, there your heart will also be."
—Matthew 6:19-21

TREASURE ENCOMPASSES TANGIBLE and intangible blessings, including real estate, resources, finances, skills, and opportunities. As we explore this topic further in the book, we will understand its significance more deeply. As stewards of treasure, we are called to acknowledge that everything we possess belongs to God and is entrusted to us for His divine purposes.

Managing our resources wisely is an essential aspect of stewardship. It requires us to steer clear of greed, the inclination to hoard, and the temptations of materialism. By doing so, we become more effective in utilizing these resources to advance God's kingdom's message, methods, and mission.

While it is true that some individuals may have been blessed with the ability to generate more incredible material wealth due to various factors such as life experiences, academic achievements, risk aversion, inheritances, or other means, the focus remains on our collective responsibility to prioritize the appropriation of our treasure for the kingdom's advancement.

A crucial part of this journey is practicing generosity and being good stewards of our resources. It involves recognizing that our resources are not solely for our benefit but are also meant to be used to meet the needs of others. By cultivating a spirit of generosity and compassion, we actively participate in the redistribution of blessings, ensuring that our treasure serves a higher purpose.

Let us explore treasure stewardship with a mindset of gratitude and a willingness to align our financial decisions and resource allocation with the principles of God's kingdom. Through intentional acts of generosity and responsible management, we can contribute to transforming lives and advancing God's purposes in the world.

Discussion Questions

1. **Reflecting on Your View of Possessions and Resources**

   a. How do you perceive your possessions and resources? Do you see them as blessings entrusted to you by God?

   _____
   _____
   _____

   b. Are there any shifts in mindset or perspective that could help you view your possessions through the lens of stewardship?

   _____
   _____
   _____

2. **Recognizing the Treasure Entrusted to Us**

   a. How can acknowledging that our possessions and resources are treasures entrusted to us by God impact our attitude and actions?

   _____
   _____
   _____

   b. In what ways does this recognition influence our decision-making and priorities?

   _____
   _____
   _____

3. **Practicing Good Stewardship of Finances and Material Possessions**
   a. What practical steps can we take to practice good stewardship of our finances?

   _____
   _____
   _____

   b. How can we intentionally use our material possessions in a way that aligns with God's purposes?

   _____
   _____
   _____

4. **Aligning Hearts with God's Kingdom**
   a. How can we ensure that our hearts are focused on God's kingdom rather than being consumed by pursuing earthly treasures?

   _____
   _____
   _____

   b. Are there any specific practices or disciplines that can help us maintain a proper perspective on possessions and resources?

   _____
   _____
   _____

More scripture to consider

Genesis 12:2 I will make you into a great nation. I will bless you and make you famous, and you will be a blessing to others NLT

Haggai 2:8 The silver is mine, and the gold is mine, saith the Lord of hosts. KJV

1 Corinthians 4:7 For what gives you the right to make such a judgment? What do you have that God hasn't given you? And if everything you have is from God, why boast as though it were not a gift? NLT

Revelation 4:10 "The four and twenty elders fall before him that sat on the throne, and worship him that liveth forever and ever, and cast their crowns before the throne, saying," KJV

In Summary

Stewardship recognizes that everything we have, including our Time, talents, and treasures, belongs to God. It involves the responsible and intentional management of these resources for God's purposes and the benefit of others. By being faithful stewards of our Time, talents, and treasures, we align ourselves with God's will and contribute to advancing His kingdom on Earth.

Discussing these questions and using scriptures as tools can deepen our understanding of kingdom stewardship and explore practical ways to align our hearts with God's kingdom. Together, we can encourage one another to adopt a stewardship mindset, practice wise management of our possessions, and seek to utilize our resources in ways that honor God and contribute to advancing His kingdom.

UNDERSTANDING KINGDOM STEWARDSHIP OF TREASURE

Stewardship refers to the responsible and ethical management, care, and protection of resources, assets, or responsibilities entrusted to an individual, group, or organization. It involves the understanding that one must act in the best interests of others and the environment to ensure the sustainability and long-term viability of the resources or responsibilities under their control.

Kingdom Stewardship of treasure is an essential aspect of our Christian walk, as it involves responsibly managing the resources and finances that God has entrusted us. It encompasses our attitudes, actions, and decisions regarding money and possessions.

Stewardship of your treasure extends beyond mere financial management. By its nature, money does not hold intrinsic value as it tends to decrease in worth over Time. Instead, true treasures are commodities that possess increasing value.

However, money can be effectively utilized to acquire these treasures and wield influence. Developing the ability and skill to use the money to leverage your efforts to pursue valuable assets is a vital aspect of responsible stewardship.

Explanation:-

God's Ownership: Recognizing that God is the ultimate owner of all things is fundamental to understanding stewardship of treasure. Everything we possess, including our financial resources, belongs to God, and we are called to manage them in a manner that honors Him.

Responsibility and Accountability: Stewardship of treasure entails recognizing our commitment to faithfully and wisely handle the resources God has given us. It involves being good stewards, making intentional choices, and being accountable to God for how we use our financial blessings.

Generosity and Kingdom Impact: Stewardship of treasure goes beyond personal gain and extends to the impact it can have on God's kingdom. It involves a willingness to share our resources generously, support the Church's work, missionary needs, meet others' needs, and advance God's purposes on Earth.

Scripture:

Matthew 6:19-21: Jesus teaches about storing treasures in heaven rather than on Earth, emphasizing the eternal value of investing in God's kingdom rather than pursuing material wealth.

2 Corinthians 9:6-8: Paul speaks about the principle of sowing and reaping, encouraging cheerful and generous giving, assuring that God blesses those who give willingly and abundantly.

Malachi 3:10: God challenges His people to bring the whole tithe into His storehouse, promising to pour blessings upon them.

Bible Study Discussion Points:

Reflect on the concept of stewardship of treasure. How does the understanding that everything we possess belongs to God impact our attitude toward money and possessions?

_____
_____
_____
_____

Discuss the importance of responsibility and accountability in managing our financial resources. How can we cultivate good stewardship habits and make wise financial decisions?

_____
_____
_____
_____

Explore the relationship between generosity and stewardship of treasure. How does giving generously align with God's heart and purposes? How can we prioritize supporting the Church's work and meeting others' needs?

_____
_____
_____
_____

Discuss personal experiences or challenges related to stewardship of treasure. How have you seen God's faithfulness when practicing good stewardship? How have you experienced growth in this area?

CHAPTER

WHAT IS KINGDOM TREASURE?

Again, the Kingdom of heaven is like unto Treasure hid in a field; when a man hath found, he hideth, and for joy thereof goeth and selleth all that he hath, and buyeth that field.
—Matthew 13:44

THE PASSAGE MENTIONED above unveils a man's extraordinary choice. This choice defies conventional norms—when he stumbled upon a treasure, he relinquished all he possessed to obtain the entire field wherein this priceless gem lay hidden.

This decision is worthy of profound attention, for it addresses a lingering question that permeates the hearts of many: why do individuals often struggle to find a deep sense of belonging within a particular nation, community, or region? The answer lies in the Treasure they unearth within that very context.

Indeed, the Treasure you uncover within a region is a profound indicator, guiding you toward where God has destined you to flourish. This Treasure can create a deep resonance within your heart, igniting an unyielding desire to connect, share, and cultivate meaningful relationships with the people and surroundings you encounter.

But the Treasure's influence extends far beyond emotional connections; it empowers you with the abundant resources, abilities, and power necessary to grow into the person you aspire to be effortlessly. Like a guiding light, it renders your vision palpable, attainable, and within arm's reach.

The significance of this revelation cannot be overstated, as it unlocks the key to an enriched and purposeful existence. By unearthing your unique Treasure, you pave the way towards genuine belonging and fulfillment—a belonging that aligns your heart with the divine plan orchestrated by the Master Craftsman, positioning you in the very place where you are meant to thrive. This profound discovery transforms a mere inhabitant into a genuine participant, actively contributing to the growth and prosperity of their surroundings.

So, dare to delve into the depths of your heart and Spirit, for therein lies the potential to unravel the Treasure that beckons you toward your destined place of belonging. Embrace the transformative power of this Treasure, for it is the guiding beacon that leads you to a life of purpose, impact, and boundless fulfillment.

Ultimately, this Kingdom treasure unfolds the divine economics of

God's Kingdom, showcasing the awe-inspiring manner in which He entrusts abundant resources to individuals, groups, or organizations. God does this to reflect His unfathomable care, protection, and acknowledgment of those who take up the mantle of responsibility for the Earth He lovingly created.

Hence, within kingdom stewardship, treasures encompass a plethora of diverse blessings and resources that God has entrusted us. These treasures are not mere trinkets; they embody profound purposes specifically tailored for lives driven by the Kingdom'sKingdom'sKingdom's call, leading to eternal fulfillment. They serve as the seeds of our mission on Earth, becoming the conduits through which our existence finds its true significance and divine purpose.

Once these treasures are discovered, our very existence transcends the limitations of earthly life. At this pivotal moment, all else becomes insignificant compared to the cultivation and development of these invaluable gifts bestowed upon us. We are left to ponder a compelling question: "Have you unearthed your treasure?" The pathway to a life of unparalleled fulfillment and eternal significance in God's Kingdom lies within its discovery.

The passage mentioned above depicts a man who, upon discovering a treasure, made the remarkable choice to sell everything he owned to purchase the entire field where the Treasure was hidden. This decision stands out because it addresses a typical inquiry: why individuals often struggle to feel a sense of belonging in a specific nation, community, or region. It suggests that a significant indicator of one's affiliation with a place or group lies in the Treasure they uncover within that context.

The Treasure you find in a region is a meaningful sign indicating where God has directed you to flourish. It can create a deep resonance within your heart, igniting a compelling desire to connect, share, and cultivate relationships. It also grants you the ability, resources, and influence to effortlessly grow into the person you aspire to be, making your vision attainable and within reach.

John 18:37 KJV Pilate said to Him, "So You are a King?" Jesus said, "You are right when you say I am a King. I was born for this reason. I came into the world for this reason. I came to speak about the truth. Everyone who is of the truth hears My voice."

They encompass tangible and intangible aspects of our lives, including relationships, talents, opportunities, material possessions, etc. It is essential to recognize that these treasures are gifts from God, and we are called to steward them effectively and responsibly.

Tangible and intangible treasures can be considered when viewing human talents as treasures.

Here are a few examples of each:

Tangible Treasures

Inventions and Innovations: Tangible creations like the light bulb, computer, or smartphone that revolutionize how we live and interact.

Artwork: Paintings, sculptures, and other artistic creations that inspire, provoke emotions, and capture the world's beauty.

Architectural Marvels: Iconic buildings and structures that showcase human creativity and engineering prowess, such as the Piramides of Egypt; the Taj Mahal in India; the Eiffel Tower of France or the Burj Khalifa, a skyscraper in Dubai, United Arab Emirates.

Scientific Discoveries: Tangible knowledge and medical, physics, or chemistry breakthroughs that lead to technological advancements and improve human life.

Written Works: Books, manuscripts, and literature that convey ideas, stories, and knowledge, preserving and sharing human experiences across generations.

Intangible Treasures

Musical Talent: The ability to compose, play an instrument, or sing, creating melodies that evoke emotions and bring joy to people's lives.

Leadership Skills: The capacity to inspire, motivate, and guide others towards a common goal, fostering collaboration and positive change.

Wisdom and Knowledge: Deep understanding, insights, and wisdom gained through experience, education, and reflection.

Empathy and Compassion: The capacity to understand and share the feelings of others, providing support and fostering connections.

Critical Thinking: The ability to analyze, evaluate, and solve complex problems, contributing to innovation, decision-making, and progress.

These are just a few examples, and human talents and treasures are vast and diverse, making each unique and capable of contributing their valuable prizes to the world. It is said that "service is the price you pay for taking up space in this world."

Treasure from God's perspective
God's Provision

Treasures manifest God's abundant provision and boundless grace in our lives. They are not haphazard or coincidental; God purposefully bestows them for our benefit. God knows you and the specific Treasure you need to live the most effective life on Earth for the Kingdom These treasures empower us to bring joy, beauty, creativity, and sustainable well-being to the Earth, allowing us to showcase and reflect God's glory in all we do.

Stewardship

Treasure is a testament to God's unwavering trust in humanity to carry out His agenda on Earth. As stewards entrusted with God's treasures, we are responsible for effectively overseeing them in His name. This entails exercising wisdom in their utilization, nurturing and fostering their growth, and ensuring they are appropriated perfectly with God's will and divine purposes. By faithfully managing these treasures, we honor God's trust in us and actively contribute to fulfilling His plans for Earth.

Multiplication and Increase

By definition, Treasure encompasses something that possesses the inherent potential to surpass its initial state and standards, destined to be utilized to expand its value. The objective of stewardship extends beyond mere preservation; it entails multiplying and increasing these treasures for the betterment of humanity. As a result, God has called and equipped us with prizes, intending to utilize them to foster their growth and multiplication, thereby bestowing blessings upon ourselves and others. We actively participate in God's plan to bring abundance and prosperity through responsible and fruitful stewardship of these treasures.

Scripture Case Study;

Matthew 25:14-30:

The parable of the Talents teaches us about the importance of stewardship. The master entrusted his servants with different amounts of talents, and those who used them wisely and multiplied them were commended and entrusted with more.

Luke 16:10: Jesus emphasizes the principle of faithfulness in managing even the most minor things entrusted to us. Being faithful with little allows us to be charged with more.

1 Peter 4:10: (Peter reminds us that each of us has received gifts from God, and we are to use them to serve one another as good stewards of God's grace.)

Luke 16:16-21 (Through Jesus' teachings, it becomes evident that treasures are not meant to be amassed and hoarded; instead, they are intended to be utilized to demonstrate richness and abundance in our relationship with God. This entails actively pursuing and fulfilling our work and assignments, serving others, and bringing glory to God in all endeavors. Utilizing our treasures this way exemplifies a deep devotion and commitment to God, showcasing His infinite goodness and grace through our actions and interactions with the world around us.)

Bible Study Discussion Points:

Reflect on the concept of treasures and their significance in our lives. How does recognizing God's provision in our blessings and resources impact our perspective and stewardship?

_____
_____
_____
_____
_____
_____
_____
_____
_____
_____

Discuss the role of stewardship in managing treasures. What does it mean to be a faithful and effective steward? How can we cultivate a stewardship mindset in various aspects of our lives?

_____
_____
_____
_____
_____
_____
_____
_____
_____

Explore examples from the Bible of individuals who effectively managed their treasures (e.g., Joseph, Daniel, Esther). What can we learn from their lives about stewardship and the blessings of faithful management?

_____
_____
_____
_____
_____
_____
_____
_____
_____
_____

Discuss potential challenges or temptations in managing treasures, such as greed, hoarding, or misusing resources. How can we overcome these challenges and maintain a perspective of stewardship?

_____
_____
_____
_____
_____
_____
_____
_____
_____
_____

CHAPTER

NATURE OF KINGDOM TREASURES

GOD'S TREASURE TOWARD us, while not exhaustive, bears immense significance, urging us to delve into the profound understanding of the nature of these precious gifts. The characteristics outlined in the list merely scratch the surface of the bountiful treasures bestowed upon us by God.

Luke 16:10-13 NLT "If you are faithful in little things, you will be faithful in large ones. But if you are dishonest in little things, you won't be honest with greater responsibilities. 11 And if you are untrustworthy about worldly wealth, who will trust you with the true riches of heaven? 12 And if you are not faithful with other people's things, why should you be trusted with things of your own? 13 "No one can serve two masters. You will hate and love one another, be devoted to one, and despise the other. You cannot serve God and be enslaved to money."

As described above, the nature of kingdom treasure or asset management highlights the principle that effective stewardship begins with faithfully managing small opportunities and resources entrusted to us. It emphasizes the importance of our character, integrity, and attitude in handling these treasures.

The nature of kingdom treasure management is such that we only sometimes start with limited resources. We may begin by managing what belongs to others. By faithfully handling these smaller treasures entrusted to us, we prove ourselves capable, faithful, and spiritually responsible for managing larger ones. Our character and integrity are vital in our promotion to the following levels.

To attract more significant opportunities, we must learn to effectively manage the small opportunities we have been given. We must approach them with a positive attitude and a commitment to honesty and integrity. Let's handle the property and responsibilities entrusted to us as if they were our own, treating them with care and respect. By doing so, we maintain a good conscience before God and ourselves, knowing we have given our best efforts to the tasks and privileges.

This poignant conversation captures the divine wisdom and foresight with which God dealt with His people as they stood on the cusp of claiming the promised Land. (Exodus 23:29 NLT But I will not drive them out in a year because the Land would become desolate and the wild animals would multiply and threaten you. I will drive them out a little at a time until your population has increased enough to take possession of the Land.)

God revealed His prudent approach: He chose not to drive out the inhabitants all at once, recognizing the potential consequences of a sudden void—desolation and a surge in wild animals that could pose a threat. Instead, God drove them out gradually, with a purposeful plan.

This act of God showcases His remarkable wisdom in handling His treasured possession, the Land, and entrusting it to the hands of His once-enslaved people. Despite their current limitations in capacity and character to govern such a vast estate, God demonstrates unwavering faith in their potential to grow and manage. He wisely prepares them for the responsibility of nurturing their population and knowledge until they are ready to possess and steward the Land effectively.

In our journeys, as we approach kingdom stewardship from God's perspective, we may encounter situations where the so-called "enemy" might unknowingly serve as an agent of God, sustaining the blessings meant for us until we are fully prepared to take possession. Just as God did with His people, He allows these circumstances to shape and refine us, instilling the necessary qualities and maturity to manage the treasures He has in store for us effectively.

The key lies in recognizing that God's timing and approach are purposeful and designed to prepare us fully for our destined inheritance. As we trust in His divine wisdom and guidance, we can rest assured that every step of the journey is intricately woven into the tapestry of His grand plan for our lives. Remember, our ability to demonstrate good stewardship and faithfully fulfill our assignments with integrity will cause the favor of God to open doors to even more excellent opportunities in the future. Let's embrace the kingdom mindset of wise stewards and seize every chance to prove ourselves trustworthy in managing big and small treasures.

CHARACTERISTICS OF TREASURES

Treasures are time-sensitive commodities.
Luke 16:3 Then the steward said within himself, What shall I do? For my Lord taketh away from me the stewardship: I cannot dig; to beg, I am ashamed.

They can be increased in value if properly managed or invested for greater return.
Luke 16:9 KJV And I say unto you, Make to yourselves friends of the mammon of unrighteousness; that, when ye fail, they may receive you into everlasting habitations.

They can be wasted.
Luke 16:1 And he also said unto his disciples, There was a confident, wealthy man, which had a steward; and the same was accused unto him that he had wasted his goods.

They can be tangible or intangible.
Luke 16:8-9 NLT "The rich man had to admire the dishonest rascal for being shrewd. And the children of this world are more shrewd in dealing with the world around them than the children of the light. 9 Here's the lesson: Use your worldly resources to benefit others and make friends. Then, when your possessions are gone, they will welcome you to an eternal home.[c]They are assets with growth potential.

They can be leveraged for greater output.
Mathew 25: 15-17 NLT He gave five bags of silver[a] to one, two bags of silver to another, and one bag of silver to the last—dividing it

proportionally to their abilities. He then left on his trip. 16 "The servant who received the five bags of silver began to invest the money and earned five more. 17 The servant with two bags of silver also went to work and earned two more.

They trust God with eventual accountability attached to them.

Luke 16:2 And he called him, and said unto him, How is it that I hear this of thee? Give an account of thy stewardship; for thou mayest be no longer steward.

KINGDOM ASSET MANAGEMENT

Starting Small: The principles of managing kingdom treasures reveal that our journey often commences with modest opportunities or resources. However, as we faithfully steward these tiny treasures in servicing God's purposes, we become eligible and entrusted with greater responsibilities and blessings. Through our diligent management of these initial gifts, we demonstrate our readiness for a more significant level in your calling, and you will experience the abundance that God graciously bestows on the faithful.

Trust and Character: In the advancement process of treasure management within the Kingdom, the character of a manager holds paramount significance. God assesses how we handle the resources entrusted to us and the integrity we exhibit in their management. Our faithfulness, responsibility, relationships, and ethical conduct in managing these resources become the focal points that determine our progression to higher levels of kingdom stewardship. Through demonstrating godly character and trustworthy management practices, we align ourselves with God's purposes and position ourselves for greater responsibilities attached to our assignment in treasury management.

Good Attitude and Honesty: When managing treasures, regardless of their size or magnitude, possessing a positive attitude and embracing honesty is essential. We are called to approach the property, enterprises, businesses, or platforms entrusted to us as if they were our very own, exemplifying a deep sense of care, responsibility, and trustworthiness.

By demonstrating such qualities in handling what has been given to us, we honor God and fulfill our assignment to be faithful stewards.

This encompasses treating the belongings and responsibilities of others with the same level of dedication and mindfulness that we would apply to our own, fostering a culture of integrity and fruitful and trustworthy relationships.

Colossians 3:23 And whatsoever ye do, do it heartily, as to the Lord, and not unto me 24 Knowing that of the Lord ye shall receive the reward of the inheritance: for ye serve the Lord Christ.

Conscience Towards God: From my perspective and firm belief, this central point stands as the foundation from which all other characteristics find genuine expression. It is an inexhaustible inspiration, fueling our sincere desire for exceptional stewardship within the Kingdom. The management of treasures encompasses our interactions with others and our deep connection with God.

We are held accountable to Him for handling and overseeing the individuals, opportunities, services, and privileges He has entrusted to our care. Nurturing a clear conscience toward God entails giving our utmost, seeking His divine guidance, and harmonizing our actions with His holy will. Through this intimate relationship with God, we discover the strength, wisdom, and grace required for remarkable stewardship, fulfilling our purpose with unwavering devotion.

Luke 12:21 So is he who layeth Treasure for himself and is not rich toward God.

KEY SCRIPTURE FOR KINGDOM ASSET MANAGERS

Luke 16:10-13 KJV 10 He that is faithful in that which is least is faithful also in much: and he that is unjust in the least is unjust also in much. 11 If therefore ye have not been faithful in the unrighteous mammon, who will commit to your trust the true riches? 12 And if ye have not been faithful in that which is another man's, who shall give you that which is your own? 13 No servant can serve two masters: for either he will hate the one, and love the other, or else he will hold to the one, and despise the other. Ye cannot serve God and mammon.

In this passage, Jesus teaches about faithfulness in small things leading to greater responsibility. He emphasizes that those faithful in little will be entrusted with much, while those dishonest in small matters will not be trusted with more fabulous treasures.)

Exodus 23:29-30 NLT But I will not drive them out in a single year, because the land would become desolate and the wild animals would multiply and threaten you. I will drive them out a little at a time until your population has increased enough to take possession of the land.

Proverbs 27:23-27 23 Be diligent to know the state of thy flocks and look well to thy herds. 24 For riches are not forever: and doth the crown endure to every generation? 25 The hay appeareth and the tender grass showeth itself, and herbs of the mountains are gathered. 26 The lambs are for thy clothing, and the goats are the price of the field. 27 And thou shalt have goats' milk enough for thy food, the food of thy household, and the maintenance for thy maidens.

1 Corinthians 4:2 NLT Now, a person in charge as a manager must be faithful.

Paul speaks about the requirement of stewards being found faithful. As stewards of God's treasures, we are called to demonstrate faithfulness in managing what has been entrusted to us.

This passage highlights the importance of diligent care and management of our resources, using the example of a shepherd tending to his flock. It underscores the value of responsible stewardship and the blessings that come from it.

Bible Study Discussion Points:

By discussing the nature of Treasure or asset management, focusing on starting minor, character, attitude, and conscience towards God, participants in the Bible study will gain a deeper understanding of the principles and qualities required for effective stewardship. They will be encouraged to approach small opportunities and resources with diligence, integrity, and a heart that seeks to honor God.

Reflect on the principle of starting small in treasury management. How does this concept challenge our perspective on opportunities and resources? How can we embrace and excel in managing tiny treasures?

___
___
___
___
___
___

Discuss the role of character and integrity in treasury management. How does our nature influence our effectiveness as stewards? Share examples from the Bible or personal experiences that illustrate the character's impact on stewardship.

_____
_____
_____
_____
_____

Explore the connection between attitude, honesty, and stewardship. How do these qualities shape our interactions with resources and opportunities? How can we cultivate a good mood and practice honesty in managing treasures?

_____
_____
_____
_____
_____

Discuss the importance of conscience towards God in treasury management. How does our accountability to God affect our approach to managing resources? How can we seek God's guidance and align our actions with His will in our stewardship?

_____
_____
_____
_____
_____

QUALITIES FOR EFFECTIVE KINGDOM TREASURE MANAGEMENT

Luke 16:10-13 KJV 10 He that is faithful in that which is least is faithful also in much: and he that is unjust in the least is unjust also in much. 11 If therefore ye have not been faithful in the unrighteous mammon, who will commit to your trust the true riches? 12 And if ye have not been faithful in that which is another man's, who shall give you that which is your own? 13 No servant can serve two masters: for either he will hate the one, and love the other, or else he will hold to the one, and despise the other. Ye cannot serve God and mammon.

Emphasizes the significance of certain qualities in kingdom treasure management, shedding light on essential attributes for effective stewardship. It is vital to recognize that the treasures entrusted to us, whether tangible or intangible, carry a divine expectation that demands our attention. As we explore various qualities, let us delve into four key attributes: faithfulness, diligence, boldness, and a steadfast commitment to continuous learning.

Faithfulness (Consistency)

In kingdom stewardship, faithfulness is vital in ensuring the effective and fruitful management of treasures. It encompasses unwavering consistency in executing our responsibilities, being dependable, and exemplifying loyalty in handling the treasures entrusted to us. Faithfulness is vital in activating God's covenant, reflecting His image and nature. God Himself is renowned as the faithful God.

By embodying faithfulness, we display our godly essence as we display dedication to our assigned task rather than seeking personal glory. Faithfulness necessitates honoring God with all our resources provided while diligently fulfilling our obligations with unwavering commitment.

Through faithfulness, we align ourselves with God's character of love and care and His purpose, and in doing so, we unleash His supernatural power that positions us for favor, fruitfulness, and fulfillment in our stewardship journey.

1 Corinthians 4:2 Now, a person in charge as a manager must be faithful. Deuteronomy 7:9—Know therefore that the LORD thy God, he is God, the faithful God, which keepeth covenant and mercy with them that love him and keep his commandments to a thousand generations;

Diligence

Diligence is crucial in effectively managing kingdom treasures, as it demands our unwavering attention and effort toward the resources entrusted to us. This encompasses being thorough and taking the information seriously. It is of utmost importance to filter all advice, opinions, contracts, and reports through the lens of God's Word.

As stewards of kingdom treasures, we must resist the temptation of separating the intellectual and spiritual realms. History attests that many profound thinkers acknowledge their wisdom to be derived from their Christian faith. Diligence serves as a shield, safeguarding us against slackness, laziness, and a careless attitude. It involves actively engaging and avoiding ignorance in our transactions, steering clear of presumptuousness.

In managing kingdom treasures, spiritual thoroughness becomes an integral component. Diligence is nourished by the Spirit of discernment, among the inspirational gifts bestowed by the Holy Spirit. Therefore, being intellectual and rational does not diminish or dilute one's spirituality. On the contrary, it enhances and deepens wisdom that would otherwise remain untapped.

By embracing diligence and discernment, we traverse our stewardship journey with wisdom, ensuring that our management of kingdom treasures remains rooted in spiritual insight and understanding.

Boldness

Being bold is significant in treasure management, mainly when dealing with limited quantities or starting from humble beginnings. It entails the courage to take initiative, seize opportunities, and step out in faith. Boldness requires placing our trust in God's provision and refraining from despising the days of small beginnings.

It opens doors to potential investments and empowers us to face challenges with unwavering courage. Undertaking elaborate ventures often demands a bold leap, which may surpass our natural inclinations.

This was the request the first church received from the Lord when they were being persecuted, and there was a threat to hinder the growth of this new movement of believers; they asked for boldness to continue spreading and becoming fruitful. Likewise, with God as our guide and source of strength, we can confidently embrace courage and venture into new territories. Through boldness, we can unlock remarkable possibilities and pursue endeavors that surpass our initial limitations.

Acts 4:29 And now, Lord, behold their threatenings: and grant unto thy servants, that with all boldness they may speak thy word,

Lifelong learning

Recognizing that our journey of kingdom stewardship is ongoing, we embrace the opportunity to grow and develop our understanding and application of managing treasures. By dedicating ourselves to lifelong learning, we demonstrate our commitment to excellence and our desire to honor God in all aspects of our stewardship journey.

A steadfast commitment to lifelong learning becomes essential in treasury management, with God as the object. Pursuing the revelations of His purpose for your life encompasses a sincere willingness to continuously improve ourselves, both spiritually and intellectually, expand our knowledge, and acquire new skills. Engaging in continuous learning empowers us to adapt to ever-changing circumstances, make informed and wise decisions, and elevate our abilities as faithful stewards. 2 Timothy 2:15 Study to shew thyself approved unto God, a workman that needeth not to be ashamed, rightly dividing the word of truth.

Key Scripture

1 Corinthians 4:2 Now, a person in charge as a manager must be faithful.

This verse emphasizes the importance of faithfulness and consistency in stewardship. It encourages us to be found faithful in managing what has been entrusted to us.

2 Peter 1:10 NLT 10 So, dear brothers and sisters,[a] work hard to prove that you really are among those God has called and chosen. Do these things, and you will never fall away.

Peter encourages believers to be diligent in their calling and work hard. Diligence leads to productivity and fruitful treasure management.

Job 8:7 NLT: Although you started with little, you will end with much.

This passage highlights the principle of not despising small beginnings. It encourages us to be bold and confident, even when starting with limited resources or opportunities.

Proverbs 13:20 NLT Walk with the wise and become wise; associate with fools and get in trouble.

Solomon teaches us the value of surrounding ourselves with wise and knowledgeable people. Continuous learning and seeking wisdom from others contribute to effective treasury management.

Bible Study Discussion Points:

Reflect on faithfulness, diligence, boldness, and continuous learning. How do these qualities contribute to effective treasury management? How have you seen these qualities displayed in your own life or the lives of others?

Discuss the challenges or obstacles that can hinder the development of these qualities in treasury management. How can we overcome these challenges and cultivate these qualities in our stewardship?

_____
_____
_____
_____
_____
_____

Explore the concept of faithfulness and consistency in stewardship. What are some practical ways we can demonstrate faithfulness in managing our treasures? How does faithfulness impact our relationship with God and others?

_____
_____
_____
_____
_____
_____

Discuss the importance of diligence in treasury management. What are some potential areas where diligence is required in stewardship? Share examples of how perseverance leads to fruitful outcomes in managing treasures.

___

By discussing the qualities of faithfulness, diligence, boldness, and continuous learning in treasure management, participants in the Bible study will gain a deeper understanding of the character traits necessary for effective stewardship. They will be encouraged to cultivate these qualities on their own.

CHAPTER

STEWARDSHIP BOOSTERS

"Have dominion"

AS WE DELVE into this Chapter, it may not be the most compelling introduction. Still, it serves as a reminder of the importance of stewardship, a concept that God first brought to the attention of Adam. Throughout our discussions, we have touched on various aspects of Time. In this Chapter, we will explore the definition and explanation of key concepts and ideas that hold significance in God's view of your stewardship.

Kingdom stewardship of Time, Talent, and Treasure, or what is commonly known in the realm of leadership as "management, involves effectively managing and utilizing the Time, Talent, and Treasure that we have been entrusted with to fulfill our responsibilities, pursue our goals, and honor God.

The phrase "have dominion" serves as a subtle reminder to Adam to keep his priorities in front of him at all times and make decisions aligned with kingdom purposes. It is not meant to trap him, as some may perceive, but rather to encourage him to structure his day to prevent failure from dominating his affairs.

By managing his (Adam's) deepest desires and resisting the temptation of distraction, he can live in alignment with God's purpose for your life. Today, we face a similar challenge as Adam did. We constantly need to manage our Time, Talent, and Treasure effectively, whether in our business endeavors, friendships, or faith environments. We are taught by the Spirit of God (1 Corinthians 2:13) that by embracing the principles of time management and prioritizing our pursuits, we can navigate these areas with achieved purpose and fulfillment.

Concept In Brief:

Recognizing Time as a Gift and Resource:

Time, a sacred blessing bestowed upon us by God, holds immense value. As stewards of the Kingdom we must cherish and utilize it wisely. We must acknowledge that Time is a creation of God, limited in nature, and should never be squandered or overlooked when God stipulates you apply your talent and treasures.

Instead, these moments we have should be revered as precious resources granting us the stage to engage and contribute to the eternal narrative. Every passing moment allows us to invest in what truly holds significance.

John 9:4 NLT *We must quickly carry out the tasks assigned to us by the one who sent us. The night is coming, and then no one can work.*

Setting Priorities: Setting priorities refers to the act of determining the relative importance or order of tasks, goals, or activities in one's life or work. It involves making conscious decisions about where to allocate one's Time, talent (energy), and treasures (resources) based on their significance, urgency, and alignment with personal or organizational objectives. Setting priorities requires thoughtful consideration and often involves evaluating different choices' potential consequences or benefits.

It helps individuals or organizations manage their Time and resources more efficiently, reduce stress, increase productivity, and achieve desired outcomes. By establishing priorities, individuals can align their actions with their long-term goals and make informed decisions about where to invest their efforts and attention.

Luke 9:15 NLT As the Time drew near for him to ascend to heaven, Jesus resolutely set out for Jerusalem.

Planning and Scheduling: Developing a well-crafted strategy and schedule empowers us to maximize our Time effectively. By setting clear goals, breaking them into manageable tasks, and organizing our activities within a program, we enhance our ability to stay focused, maintain order, and boost productivity.

While human inclination may lead us to rely solely on statistics or prevailing societal circumstances when creating plans, as stewards of the Kingdom, we possess the remarkable advantage of accessing divine wisdom and understanding (1 Corinthians 1:24). This enables us to construct exceptional frameworks and systems incomparable with the world that pave the way for success.

Luke 14:28 "But begin once you count the cost. Who would start building construction without first calculating the cost to see if there is enough money to finish it?

Eliminating Time Wasters: Effective time management entails recognizing and eliminating activities or habits that deplete our Time without adding value or aligning with our priorities. In Scripture, the enemy is referred to as a destroyer who steals, kills, and destroys (John 10:10). It is intriguing to note that not all time wastage can be attributed to the enemy's influence, yet the loss of Time can feel profoundly distressing and result in a significant reduction in blessings.

Consequently, overcoming challenges such as excessive indulgence in entertainment, social media, or other distractions impeding productivity is crucial in minimizing time wastage. As mentioned earlier, Time is an exceedingly valuable commodity, and since it cannot be regulated or conserved, utilizing it wisely is paramount. At the same time, any other use of it leads to waste.

1 Corinthians 10:23 All things are lawful for me, but all things are not expedient: all things are lawful for me, but all things edify not.

Practicing Discipline and Self-Control:

Practicing discipline involves consistently adhering to rules, routines, or principles to achieve personal or professional goals. It requires conscious decision-making, effective task prioritization, and efficient allocation of Time and resources. Similarly, self-control refers to managing and regulating one's emotions, desires, impulses, and behaviors, restraining oneself from immediate gratification that could hinder long-term goals or values.

These symbiotic concepts are vital for successful kingdom stewards who seek fruitfulness in managing kingdom time, talent, and Treasure.

Intentionally cultivating and managing discipline and self-control are necessary to fully access God's favor. As Apostle Paul wisely stated in

1 Corinthians 10:23 NLT You say, "I am allowed to do anything" [a]—but not everything is good for you. You say, "I am allowed to do anything,"—but not everything is beneficial.

Refraining from following the practice of discipline or self-control often leads to procrastination when implementing important decisions or commands from the Lord. Procrastination can become a frustrating pattern in life if left unchecked. Furthermore, discipline and self-control are not isolated concepts; they are precious fruits of a spirit-filled life. As kingdom stewards, we are invited to embrace growth by allowing these fruits to nurture and develop us into effective stewards.

In managing Time, Talent, and Treasure, accessing the gifts of the Spirit, such as temperance and self-control (Galatians 5:22), becomes essential in remaining committed to our priorities. This involves prioritizing activities like starting the day with prayer, reading spiritual blogs, deep meditation by confessing God's words or listening to podcasts, and short spirit-inspired videos during daily routines.

These practices reinforce our submission to the Kingdom's purpose. It may also require making sacrifices, confidently saying "no" to certain activities, and establishing healthy boundaries to maintain focus and alignment with our goals.

Seeking God's Guidance: Guidance refers to receiving direction, advice, or assistance in making decisions, navigating challenges, or pursuing a desired course of action. It involves seeking and receiving support from trusted sources, such as mentors, experts, or spiritual leaders, who provide insight and wisdom based on their knowledge and experience.

The purpose of the guidance is to provide clarity, wisdom, and direction when faced with uncertainty or complexity. It helps individuals make informed choices, avoid pitfalls, and maximize their potential for success. Guidance can also offer encouragement, validation, and reassurance during challenging times, boosting confidence and resilience.

God's guidance is not just a choice; it is an absolute necessity, as emphasized by Jesus in *John 15:5 NLT: "I am the vine; you are the branches. Those who remain in me, and I in them, will bear much fruit. Apart from me, you can do nothing."* We must acknowledge this truth and actively seek God's guidance. God possesses complete knowledge and understanding, seeing the end from the beginning. Moreover, He has an unwavering belief in the success of our endeavors, far beyond what we can comprehend.

Recognizing our limitations as humans is essential, as our knowledge is inherently limited. This realization highlights the urgent need to seek God's guidance. God graciously invites us to allow His voice to lead us to fulfillment. As Kingdom Stewards, our approach should be humble, understanding that it is not about our plans and ambitions but about aligning our Time, talents, and resources with God's divine will.

Through prayer, studying His Word, and being attuned to the promptings of the Holy Spirit, we actively pursue and receive God's guidance. This enables us to make choices that align with His purposes and bring honor to Him through our stewardship. By surrendering to God's guidance, we acknowledge His wisdom, trust His direction, and invite Him to guide our paths.

SCRIPTURE REFERENCE

Ecclesiastes 3:1-2—*"For everything, there is a season, and a time for every matter under heaven: a time to be born, and a time to die; a time to plant, and a time to pluck up what is planted."* This verse reminds us of the seasons of life and the importance of discerning the right Time for different activities.

Ephesians 5:15-16—*"Look carefully then how you walk, not as unwise but as wise, making the best use of the time because the days are evil."* This verse highlights the need to make wise choices and utilize our Time effectively in a world that can easily distract and deceive us.

Psalm 90:12—*"So teach us to number our days that we may get a heart of wisdom."* This prayer of Moses reminds us of the brevity of life and the importance of using our Time wisely. It prompts us to seek God's guidance in stewarding our Time.

Proverbs 16:9—*"The heart of man plans his way, but the LORD establishes his steps."* This verse reminds us to make plans and set goals and trust in God's sovereignty and guidance in directing our paths.

Psalms 32:8 NLT The Lord says, "I will guide you along the best pathway for your life. I will advise you and watch over you.

Discussion Questions:

How have you experienced the impact of effective time management in your life? Share specific examples of how managing your Time well has brought positive results.

_____
_____
_____
_____

What are some common challenges or obstacles you face in managing your Time effectively? How can you overcome these challenges with the help of God's wisdom and strength?

_____

_____

_____

_____

_____

How can seeking God's guidance and aligning our Time with His will bring greater purpose and fulfillment to our daily activities?

_____

_____

_____

_____

_____

Share practical strategies or tips to help us manage our Time more effectively. How can we prioritize our tasks, eliminate time-wasting activities, and stay disciplined in following our schedules?

_____

_____

_____

_____

_____

Remember, the goal of this study is not only to gain practical strategies for time management but also to develop a mindset and heart that align with God's perspective on Time, Talent, and Treasure. Let the discussion and insights from this study prompt personal reflection and action in stewardship more effectively for God's purposes.

HINDRANCES TO STEWARDSHIP

As we reflect on the Kingdom of God, let's delve into hindrances that can obstruct our effectiveness in stewarding God's plans and purposes. Several obstacles can hinder our utilization of Time, talent, and resources. Specifically, we will examine slothfulness, laziness, procrastination, and excuses within a Bible study, drawing insights and wisdom from relevant scriptures.

SLOTHFULNESS

Romans 12:11 KJV Not slothful in business; fervent in Spirit; serving the Lord;

Slothfulness is characterized by being lazy, inactive, or needing more diligence. It manifests as a lack of drive, motivation, or enthusiasm to engage in productive activities or fulfill one's responsibilities. Those who are slothful tend to avoid putting in effort or taking initiative, often opting for idleness or procrastination.

Slothfulness hampers personal growth, inhibits the pursuit of excellence, and obstructs the effective utilization of Time and abilities. It is essential to differentiate slothfulness from genuine rest or relaxation, as it involves a chronic avoidance of necessary tasks and a lack of proactive engagement with the demands of life. In the Bible, slothfulness is a negative attribute hindering productivity.

Proverbs 24:30 NLT I walked by the field of a lazy person, the vineyard of one with no common sense. 31 I saw that it was overgrown with nettles. It was covered with weeds, and its walls were broken down. 32 Then, as I looked and thought about it, I learned this lesson: 33 A little extra sleep, a little more slumber, a little folding of the hands to rest—34 then poverty will pounce on you like a bandit; scarcity will attack you like an armed robber.

Interestingly, many may attribute exerting energy to being a workaholic. Still, it is good to stress that it is possible to exert power at your work but not be a workaholic. Some people work hard at their work, but workaholics have no control over what they do; they are overwhelmed with the thought that stepping away means the end of the project, as it were.

Workaholics find joy in the work itself, while working hard means that the laborer has a grip on their Time and can easily step away and allow for rest and recovery. But it is wise to consider the other end of the spectrum where your stewardship is concerned n to become slack in thinking that not exerting Time and effort will amount to favor with God. The Scripture never glorified slothfulness in any way as a matter of Jesus revealing our Father in heaven who works:

John 5:17 NLT Jesus replied, "My Father is always working, and so am I."
Proverbs 18:9 KJV "One who is slack in his work is brother to one who destroys.

PROCRASTINATION

Proverbs 13:4 "The appetite of the sluggard craves and gets nothing, while the appetite of the diligent is richly supplied."

Procrastination is delaying or postponing tasks or decisions, often due to a lack of motivation, fear of failure, or poor time management skills. It can lead to increased stress, decreased productivity, and missed deadlines.

Procrastination refers to delaying or postponing tasks or actions that need to be completed. It involves intentionally putting off or avoiding work, often favoring more immediate and pleasurable activities. Procrastination is often driven by a desire to avoid discomfort, fear of failure, lack of motivation, or difficulty initiating tasks. It can result in a loss of productivity, increased stress, missed deadlines, and negatively impact one's overall well-being. Procrastination can be a habit or a pattern of behavior that interferes with effective time management and goal achievement.

EXCUSES

Excuses are rationalizations or justifications we give ourselves or others for not completing tasks or fulfilling commitments. Making excuses allows us to avoid taking responsibility and can hinder our ability to manage Time effectively.

Scripture: Luke 14:16-20

"Jesus replied: 'A certain man was preparing a great banquet and invited many guests. At the Time of the banquet, he sent his servant to tell those invited, "Come, for everything is now ready." But they all alike began to make excuses. The first said, "I have just bought a field, and I must go and see it. Please excuse me." Another said, "I have just bought five yokes of oxen, and I'm on my way to try them out. Please excuse me." Still, another said, "I just got married, so I can't come."'

These hindrances to time management are cautioned against in the Bible, emphasizing the importance of diligence, discipline, and taking responsibility for our actions. By acknowledging and addressing these hindrances, we can strive for greater productivity and stewardship of the Time entrusted to us.

Discussion questions

How do you struggle with slothfulness, laziness, procrastination, or making excuses when managing your time effectively?

_____
_____
_____
_____

What are some specific tasks or areas of your life where you tend to procrastinate or make excuses?

_____
_____
_____
_____

Are there any biblical principles or verses that have helped you overcome these hindrances to time management?

_____
_____
_____
_____

How can we support and encourage one another to develop better time management habits and overcome these hindrances?

_____
_____
_____
_____

These hindrances to time management are cautioned against in the Bible, emphasizing the importance of diligence, discipline, and taking responsibility for our actions. By acknowledging and addressing these hindrances, we can strive for greater productivity and stewardship of the Time entrusted to us.

Recognize the importance of seeking God's wisdom in managing your Time effectively. Set aside Time for prayer and reflection to seek God's guidance in prioritizing your tasks and responsibilities.

Proverbs 3:5-6 KJV *"Trust in the LORD with all your heart and lean not on your understanding; in all your ways submit to him, and he will make your paths straight."*

TOOLS FOR COMBATING HINDRANCES

SET GOALS AND CREATE A SCHEDULE

Psalm 90:12 KJV "Teach us to number our days, that we may gain a heart of wisdom."

Set measurable goals for various areas of your life, such as work, family, and personal growth. Create a schedule or to-do list to help you allocate Time for different activities and tasks. "Number my days" means taking charge of your stewardship. Setting measurable goals and organizing your Time through a schedule or to-do list brings structure and clarity to your life. The design is critical to being led effectively by the Spirit. This approach allows you to track your progress, stay focused on your objectives, and make steady strides toward personal growth and success in all areas of life. Regularly review and adjust your goals and schedule as circumstances change, and always be kind to yourself during the process, acknowledging that progress may not always be linear. With dedication and consistency, you can lead a more fulfilling and balanced life.

SET YOURSELF ON FIRE

Romans 12:11 KJV Not slothful in business; fervent in Spirit; serving the Lord;
Start by taking immediate action on vital tasks to conquer the inclination to procrastinate. Cultivate a fiery desire within yourself, fueled by the Time, Talent, and Treasure you've uncovered. Just as fire doesn't wait, be proactive and determined in your pursuits.

Develop a consistent prayer life to reinforce your aspirations and regularly engage with scriptures that remind you of your goals. Let desire ignite your mind, fostering a diligent work ethic, and driving you to pursue excellence in every endeavor.

PRACTICE SELF-DISCIPLINE AND AVOID DISTRACTIONS:

1 Corinthians 9:24-25 NLT "Do you not know that all the runners run in a race, but only one gets the prize? Run in such a way as to get the prize. Everyone who competes in the games goes into strict training. They do it to get a crown that will not last, but we do it to get one that will last forever."

Develop the self-discipline to focus on your tasks and avoid distractions that can waste Time, Talent, and Treasure. Set boundaries with technology, social media, and other potential distractions. Stay on your lane! The

DELEGATE AND SEEK SUPPORT

Ecclesiastes 4:9 "Two are better than one because they have a good return for their labor."

Learn to delegate tasks when appropriate and seek support from others when needed. Cultivate a spirit of collaboration and recognize that you do not have to carry all the responsibilities alone.

REST AND PRIORITIZE SELF-CARE

Mark 6:31 "Then, because so many people were coming and going that they did not even have a chance to eat, he said to them, 'Come with me by yourselves to a quiet place and get some rest.'

Recognize the importance of rest and self-care in maintaining productivity and overall well-being. Set aside time for relaxation, recreation, and spiritual nourishment.

Discussion questions

What strategies have you found helpful in your tasks and responsibilities?

How do you stay motivated and avoid procrastination when faced with challenging or less enjoyable tasks?

Are there any biblical principles or scriptures that have guided you in managing your time effectively?

How can we support and hold one another accountable in our pursuit of effective time management?

How can we ensure that our time management practices align with our values and priorities as followers of Christ?

THE ATTITUDE OF A WILLING HEART

RECOGNIZING THAT WE ARE STEWARDS OF GOD'S GRACE

The attitude of a willing heart and recognizing that we are stewards of God's grace are vital aspects of our response to God's call to use our Time, Talents, and Treasure. When we approach the deployment of our gifts with a willing and surrendered heart, acknowledging that we are stewards of God's grace, we position ourselves to fulfill our purpose and bring glory to Him.

Explanation:

Willing Heart: A generous heart means being open and receptive to God's leading and guidance in using our Time, Talent, and Treasures. It involves surrendering our desires and agendas, allowing God to direct us in utilizing our gifts for His purposes best. 1 Corinthians 15:31 I protest by your rejoicing which I have in Christ Jesus our Lord, I die daily.

Stewards of God's Grace: Recognizing that we are stewards of God's grace means understanding that our Time, Talent, and Treasures are entrusted to us by God. We are not the owners but rather caretakers of these gifts. We must use them wisely and faithfully, knowing they are ultimately given to us to advance God's Kingdom.

Scripture:

1 Peter 4:10-11: Peter reminds us that our gifts are given to us by God's grace, and we are to use them to serve others faithfully, administering God's grace in its various forms.

Exodus 35:29: This verse describes the response of the Israelites when contributing their talents and skills to the construction of the Tabernacle. They gave willingly and with wholehearted devotion, recognizing that they were contributing to the work of the Lord.

2 Corinthians 9:7: Paul encourages cheerful giving, emphasizing that God loves a person who presents with a willing heart, not reluctantly or under compulsion.

Bible Study Discussion Points:

Reflect on the meaning of having a willing heart. How does a generous heart impact our attitude and actions when using our talents for God's purposes?

Discuss the concept of stewardship about our talents. What does it mean to be a steward of God's grace? How does this perspective shape our approach to deploying our gifts?

Explore biblical examples of individuals who demonstrated a willing heart and recognized themselves as stewards of God's grace (e.g., the parable of the talents in **Matthew 25:14-30,** the story of Bezalel and Oholiab in **Exodus 31:1-11).** What can we learn from their attitudes and actions?

Discuss any challenges or barriers that may hinder us from having a willing heart or embracing our role as stewards of God's grace. How can we overcome these obstacles and cultivate a spirit of surrender and obedience?

CONCLUSION

IN THIS BOOK, we have embarked on a journey into stewardship, exploring the various dimensions of Time, Talent, Treasure, and the seasons of life. Throughout our study, we have gained a deeper understanding of God's desire for us to be faithful stewards of all He has entrusted to us.

We have learned that kingdom stewardship is not just about managing our resources but about recognizing that everything we have comes from God. It is a call to honor Him with our Time, talents, and treasures, seeking to align our lives with His purposes and glorify Him in all we do.

We have examined the importance of discovering and developing our talents, recognizing that we have unique gifts and abilities ready to be used for God's Kingdom. We have seen the value of good stewardship in managing our financial resources and acknowledging that everything we possess ultimately belongs to God.

Furthermore, we have explored the concept of Time as a precious and limited resource. We have been challenged to use our Time wisely, number our days, and seek God's guidance in managing each moment; He has given us. We have discovered that effective time management leads to productivity and allows us to invest in what truly matters—our relationship with God and the well-being of others.

Additionally, we have examined the different seasons of life—the learning years, earning years, and yearning years and how each season presents unique opportunities and challenges. We have been encouraged to embrace and maximize each phase, trusting that God has a purpose for every season and that He is with us through each transition.

As we conclude this book, let us remember that stewardship is not a one-time endeavor but a lifelong journey. It requires intentionality, discipline, and a heart surrendered to God. It is a daily commitment to seek His wisdom, follow His guidance, and rely on His strength in managing all aspects of our lives.

May we continue to grow in our understanding of stewardship and live in a way that brings glory to God. Let us support and encourage one another as we strive to be faithful stewards, positively impacting our families, communities, and world.

May the lessons we have learned in this book inspire us to live lives of purpose, generosity, and love, knowing that as we faithfully steward what God has entrusted to us, He will continue to guide, bless, and transform us for His glory.

May God grant us the grace to be faithful stewards, now and forever.
Amen.

OTHER RESOURCES FROM THE AUTHOR

Complete or Compete
Know Yourself
Fire Rain

www.ingramcontent.com/pod-product-compliance
Lightning Source LLC
LaVergne TN
LVHW061551070526
838199LV00077B/7000